UNDERSTANDING
FINANCIAL
STEWARDSHIP

CHARLES
STANLEY

OLIVER NELSON

THOMAS NELSON PUBLISHERS
Nashville • Atlanta • London • Vancouver

Published in Nashville, Tennessee, by Thomas Nelson, Inc., Publishers, and distributed in Canada by Word Communications, Ltd., Richmond, British Columbia.

The Bible version used in this publication is THE NEW KING JAMES VERSION. Copyright © 1979, 1980, 1982, Thomas Nelson, Inc., Publishers.

ISBN 0-7852-7274-7

Printed in the United States of America.

CONTENTS

WHAT IS YOUR NET WORTH?

Net worth is a concept that most people understand solely in terms of finance—it refers to the numerical figure remaining after your debts have been subtracted from your assets. Ideally, the amount is a positive number, not a negative one. The larger the number, the richer you are thought to be from a human perspective.

Net worth from God's perspective is different. God sees the whole of your life when He views your prosperity. He doesn't divide your life into segments and evaluate you according to some kind of average of strengths and weaknesses. More important, God doesn't look at any numbers or other statistics when He calculates your worth. He looks instead at His immeasurable love for you and the sacrifice that Jesus Christ made on the cross. In that light, you are beyond any measurement that might be associated with value. (See John 3:16.)

Fully Vested for Prosperity

Once you have accepted Jesus Christ as your Savior and have received God's forgiveness for your sin, you are fully vested in God's total prosperity plan. You qualify fully for His promises related to prosperity and blessing.

That isn't the case for nonbelievers. People who have not accepted Jesus Christ simply cannot experience full prosperity— according to God's definition of prosperity—primarily because being prosperous includes prosperity in the spiritual life.

You must understand these key concepts at the outset of this study about financial stewardship and prosperity:

1. Prosperity relates to your entire life. A person can be rich and still not be prosperous. When you think of blessing and prosperity, you must think in terms of life's whole—a harmony that has spiritual, mental, emotional, physical, financial, and relational dimensions.

2. Prosperity is God's plan for every believer. God's greatest desire is that you be a whole person. He desires to bless you and cause you to grow in every area of your life in a balanced and fruitful way. He desires for you to fulfill His destiny for you on this earth—and to do so as a whole person. God wants you to prosper.

It is with this frame of mind that you should approach the subject of financial stewardship.

Financial Stewardship

Financial stewardship has to do with the way in which you use your resources to provide for your needs and for the needs of God's kingdom on this earth. Stewardship involves far more than your money. Why? Because your resources involve far more than money and material goods. Among your resources are your talents, abilities, capabilities, skills, experiences, creative ideas, energy, time, strength, spiritual gifts, and much more. Your resources encompass the total you. Just as God desires to bless all of you and to be directly involved in every area of your life, so God desires for all of you to be actively involved in His plan for this world.

God has given you all that you have and all of your potential. All that you are and all that you will ever be are His gifts to you. His desire is that you will desire to give back to Him all that you are and all that you hope to be.

I have labeled this study *financial stewardship* for two reasons:

First, we are focusing on *material and financial resources.* That certainly doesn't mean that stewardship is limited to finances. But a complete study of stewardship would require far more than this one Bible study book can contain.

Second, this study is concerned with *stewardship*, not merely finances. Stewardship involves all of the giving and receiving principles that apply to your relationship with God and your support of God's purposes and plan for your life and the lives of others. Stewardship implies a caretaker role. A good steward manages the resources of the master with the utmost care and concern.

Every person is a steward of God's gifts, including money and material goods. Therefore, financial stewardship is something with which all people are involved whether they know it or not. You are a financial steward for your Master and Lord, Jesus Christ. If you have never thought of yourself in that role before, I invite you to see yourself in that role today.

God has a perfect plan for what you are to do with your money and material wealth. He has a plan for blessing you with an increase in money and material possessions, and for you to increase your ability to bless others. The goal in this study is to help you discover that plan of God.

No Separation

Many people have a mind-set that "business is business" and "church is church." They separate the two almost completely in their minds and sometimes in the way they act. They have differing attitudes toward money and toward worship. It may come as quite a jolt to your thinking to face the reality of God's Word: God doesn't separate your business life from your spiritual life. The two are vitally and intricately connected.

Again, we go back to our understanding of prosperity. You simply cannot be prosperous if you are succeeding, growing, and bearing fruit in only one area of your life. Prosperity has to do with all your life. In a very practical way, God is just as concerned about your finances and your ability to meet your physical and material needs as He is with your spiritual growth and development.

Many people have been taught—incorrectly, I hasten to add—

to think of money as being filthy lucre. They view finance and business as unspiritual matters, and certainly not anything that could ever be considered holy. They regard money and financial principles as subjects that should be outside the domain of the church.

Let me assure you, God doesn't see money as filthy. Money itself is neutral in His eyes. It is what we do with our money that counts before God. His desire is that our financial life become sanctified, which means that we deal with our finances in purity, governed by right motives, and in ways that are wholly acceptable to God.

Furthermore, if church leaders had taught people through the years more about good financial stewardship based on principles in God's Word, many people would have been spared heartache and sorrow.

As a pastor, I have talked to or corresponded with thousands of people over the years who have shared with me their problems and difficulties. A very large percentage of the problems have been rooted in financial difficulty, have been compounded by financial difficulty, or have resulted in financial difficulty.

Many people who have marital difficulties readily admit that their difficulties involve money. Others are heartbroken that they aren't prepared for retirement, unexpected illness, or major financial expenditures—such as helping a child with college—because they have never learned to manage their money according to God's principles. Still others are frustrated that they seem to be unable to do the ministry work that God has called them to do because they don't have the resources to meet their needs or the needs of their ministries—again, because they aren't living according to God's principles of sound financial stewardship.

One thing I know about financial difficulties—they affect all other areas of a person's life. You cannot have a major problem or crisis involving money and not experience some degree of difficulty, doubt, or frustration in your mind, emotions, and relationships, including your relationship with God.

It is a good, right, and scriptural undertaking to talk about money and to discover what God has to say about its acquisition and use. It is good for you, and it is good for the church as a whole, to know God's will for the material life.

For Your Blessing

I've also discovered through the years that the minute a preacher begins to talk about money, many people jump to a conclusion that the preacher wants their money. Furthermore, they tend to hold a suspicion that the preacher wants their money for his use. Let me assure you at the very outset of this study that I don't want anything *from* you. At no time in this study will I ask you for a contribution or financial gift. Instead, I want something *for* you.

I want to see you blessed fully by God. I want to see you become a whole person and be prosperous in every area of your life. I want to see you fulfill your purpose on this earth. I want to help you understand God's principles for good financial stewardship so you can begin to use them—for your benefit.

I know that when you are blessed and truly understand God's plan, you will desire to give, but the ministry to which you give, the amount you give, and the frequency with which you give are going to be strictly between you and God.

God's principles for financial stewardship and prosperity are universal, eternal, and absolute. The specific ways in which God directs you to use your resources and to give of yourself are going to be equally personal, detailed, and specific.

Trust God to be true to His Word.

Trust Him to bless you.

Trust Him to guide your stewardship of the gifts He gives you.

Let God be the Provider for your entire life, including your finances, and the Source of your prosperity.

PREPARING FOR A FRESH LOOK AT FINANCIAL STEWARDSHIP

Many people think of the Bible as being only a book of inspiration and spiritual truths. It certainly is that. But the Bible is also one of the most practical, down-to-earth books that has ever been written. It relates to every area of our lives, including the acquisition and use of money and material possessions.

The Bible has a great deal to say about wealth and poverty, and what makes a person rich or poor. It contains eternal truths about the importance of giving, the necessity of receiving, and the way to prosperity.

I have found in my ministry that people tend to have two difficulties when it comes to what the Bible has to say about money.

First, they tend to focus on what people have told them the Bible says rather than what the Bible actually says. Or they quote one verse or portion of a verse out of context and take that as the entire biblical opinion on the subject. In this study, I encourage you to let the Bible speak for itself.

Second, people tend to question whether what the Bible says is applicable to them. They say, "I know that's what the Bible says, but is this really true for me? Can I trust God to do this in my life? How does this relate to my life today?"

Let me assure you that God's Word is for you, and it is for your life right now. God's truth is not bound to any one era or limited to any one classification of person. There are truths in God's Word that are exclusively for God's people—those who have accepted Jesus Christ as their Savior and are trusting in God with all the heart, mind, and soul—but an equal truth is that every person has an open invitation to become one of God's people! No promise or principle of God is off-limits to a person's ability to conform to it, receive it, or act upon it.

As you study God's principles for good financial stewardship, I encourage you to go again and again to your Bible and to underline phrases, highlight words or verses, and make notes in the margins of your Bible to record the specific ways God speaks to you. I believe in a well-marked Bible. My Bible is filled with dates, notes, and insights.

God's truth is for all people at all times, but the application of that truth to your life is always very personal and direct. Take note of the specific ways in which God admonishes, encourages, or directs you.

For Personal or Group Study

The book you hold can be used by you alone or by several people for a small-group study. If you are using this book for a personal Bible study, you will find places from time to time in which to note your insights or to respond to questions that are asked. If you are using the book for a small-group study, you also may use these questions and insight portions for group discussion.

At various times, you will be asked to relate to the material in one of these ways:

- What new insights have you gained?
- Have you ever had a similar experience?
- How do you feel about the material presented?
- In what way do you feel challenged to respond or to act?

Insights

An insight is more than a mere fact or idea. It is seeing something as if it is new to you. Most of us have had the experience of reading a passage of the Bible—perhaps even a passage that we have read dozens of times—and saying, "I never saw that before. I've never noticed that particular word or phrase. I have an entirely new understanding of that story or teaching." You may have studied or meditated on the passage in the past, but suddenly, God reveals a deeper level of meaning to you. That is a spiritual insight.

Your insights are likely to be individualized and are very often related to your personal life. You tend to see things in a new light as God's Word relates to something you are currently experiencing or have just encountered. At other times, an insight helps you pull it all together as you reflect on a relationship, experience, or incident. At still other times, an insight answers a question for you, and you have a sudden knowing about what to do, how to think, or why you believe what you believe.

Ask the Lord to speak to you personally every time you open His Word. I believe He will be faithful in answering your prayer. I also believe the insights He gives you will arouse greater enthusiasm for your study of His Word.

As you experience insights, make notes about them. You may want to make these notes in your Bible or in a separate journal. The more you record insights, the more you are likely to have insights. In other words, the more you look and listen for God to speak to you, the more He does! In fact, if you haven't gained new spiritual insights after reading several passages from God's Word, you probably haven't been engaged in the process of study.

From time to time in this book, you will be asked to note what a passage of the Bible is saying to you. These are times for recording your personal response or insight, not for summarizing a group response or what someone else in your Bible study group said. Make sure the insight or response is your own.

Experience

Each of us comes to God's Word from a unique background. Nobody else has our particular set of experiences, relationships, or contexts for learning. Each of us has a bank of ideas, opinions, and emotions. Therefore, each of us has a unique perspective on what is read in God's Word.

Differing levels of experience can create problems in group Bible studies, although this is not necessarily so. People who have gone to church all their lives and have heard the Bible stories and good preaching for many years are likely to have a different depth of understanding of God's Word from that of people who are new Christians or who have never read the Bible. In a group setting, these differences can cause a beginner to feel lost or an old-timer to feel impatient.

What we do have in common are life experiences. We can point to times in which we have found the Bible to be applicable to us—perhaps in a convicting, challenging way, perhaps in an encouraging, comforting way. We have had experiences about which we can say, "Here's how that truth in the Bible displayed itself in my life," or "Here's what happened to me to convince me that God's Word is true."

Of course, our experiences do not make the Bible true. The Bible is truth. The importance of noting and sharing our experiences is that we discover the many ways in which God's truth can be applied to human lives and circumstances. In sharing our life experiences, we see how God speaks personally and directly to each person. We see how His Word applies to practical needs, questions, and situations. We begin to discover that God's Word is not only universal, but also very specific. We nearly always come to the conclusion that our greatest potential for harmony and unity lies in each person having a relationship with Christ Jesus and a desire to live according to God's principles. The Lord and His Word tie us together with bonds that cannot be broken.

Sharing experiences is significant for spiritual growth. If you are doing this study on your own, find someone with whom you can share your faith experiences. Be open to hearing about that person's faith experiences in return.

Emotional Response

Just as each of us has a personal catalog of life experiences, so each of us has a set of emotional responses. We need to allow others to share their emotional responses to God's Word without judgment or comment. You may be overjoyed or feel encouraged after reading a particular passage in the Bible. Another person may respond to that same passage with fear, perplexity, or doubt.

Face your emotions honestly. Learn to share your emotional responses with others.

You may think, *Money isn't an emotional subject, such as love, joy, or peace. Finance is a cut-and-dried subject.*

In my experience, money is one of the most emotion-laden subjects I've ever encountered. How do you feel at these times:

- When you discover that you are overdrawn in your checking account?
- When you face the possibility that you have bills you may never be able to pay?
- When you get a raise or bonus?
- When you are told that the repair, or service, is going to cost far more than you had anticipated?
- When you receive an unexpected windfall or inheritance?

Even if you haven't been through each of the experiences above, you likely can imagine fairly accurately what your emotional response would be. A lack of prosperity causes you to feel discouraged, fearful, doubtful, anxious, and frustrated. Total provision and prosperity cause you to feel elated, joyful, energetic, creative, hopeful, satisfied, and fulfilled.

Emotional responses don't give validity to the Scriptures. Nor should you trust emotions as a measuring device for your faith. Your faith is to be based on what God says, not on how you feel.

Just because you like a particular story or passage of the Bible doesn't make it more true or more helpful than another passage. You must be balanced in your understanding of your emotions: on the one hand, you do have an emotional response to God's Word; on the other, you must not let your emotions rule your interpretation of God's Word or limit your reading of God's Word only to the passages that make you feel happy and hopeful. You must not allow yourself to concentrate solely on God's promises of provision without also taking into full consideration God's warnings about money and possessions.

In most small-group settings, I have found it much more beneficial for people to express their emotions rather than their opinions. Some of the ways in which God speaks to us through His Word are nonverbal. The Holy Spirit often speaks to us in the unspoken language of promptings, intuition, emotions, and deep desires and longings. When we share these feelings with one another, we not only open ourselves to deeper insights into God's Word but also grow closer together as members of the body of Christ. A sense of community develops, and we understand more clearly what it means to be "one in the Spirit." It is through the sharing of joys and sorrows, assurances and doubts, hopes and fears, that we mature as individuals and as churches.

Challenges

As we read God's Word, we nearly always feel conviction at some point—as if God is speaking directly to us. I once heard a person say, "God has my name on that verse." That's the way a conviction or a challenge may seem to you.

God's Word causes you to feel challenged to change something in your life, to take a new step, or to make a fresh start. At times you may feel challenged to stand firm or to continue steadfastly in the direction you are going. These moments of conviction can be very strong. They may occur once or repeatedly, but they are virtually impossible to escape or ignore.

The more practical the subject matter, the stronger the convictions seem to be. Perhaps that is because God's message and meaning are so clear that there is little room to justify, explain away, or misinterpret what God is saying to you.

I am saying all of this to alert you to the fact that as you study what God's Word says about financial stewardship, you are likely to feel challenged or convicted in rather powerful ways. Your first impulse may be to close your Bible, close this book, and walk away—either elated or deflated! Don't give in to that impulse. Stay with your study and get the whole of God's message. Make sure your final decision to take action is based on a complete understanding of God's principles and plan.

I believe we gain a great deal by writing down the ways in which we believe God is stretching us, molding us, calling us, or causing us to believe for more. When we identify clearly and succinctly what God wants us to do and why, we are in a much better position to take action that is responsible, measured, and deliberate. We are to *respond* to God's Word, not merely react to it.

Ultimately, God desires to get His Word into us and us into His Word so we can take His Word into the world, live it out, and be witnesses of His Word in all we say and do. We are to be God's living letters on financial stewardship to others. It is not enough for us to note our insights, recall our past experiences, share our emotions, or write down the ways in which we feel challenged. We must actually do what God calls us to do. We must obey God's Word and be doers of it. (See James 1:22.)

Very specifically, it isn't enough for you to become financially savvy and to know all of God's principles that relate to money and material goods. You must do what God says to do. You must become the good steward that He is calling you to be.

Keep the Bible Central

Again, I caution you to keep the Bible at the center of your study. Otherwise, your group may become a therapy or support group of some type—or in the case of this topic, a group that gives financial tips and money-managing advice. You must also guard against a tendency in your group to complain about a lack of prosperity or to brag about ways in which God has blessed you.

Therapy, support, and information-sharing groups have their time and place, but in the end, it is as we gather around God's Word—to feed upon it, learn from it, and grow into it—that we truly grow spiritually and put ourselves into a position of total prosperity, a prosperity based on prosperity of spirit.

If you are doing a personal Bible study, you also must be diligent in staying focused on God's Word. Self-analysis and introspection are not the goals of this study. Growing into the fullness of the stature of Christ Jesus is the goal!

Prayer

I encourage you to begin and end your Bible study sessions in prayer. Ask God to give you spiritual eyes to see what He wants you to see and spiritual ears to hear what He wants you to hear. Ask Him to give you new insights, to recall to your memory the experiences that are helpful to your growth, and to help you identify your emotions with clarity. Be bold and ask Him to reveal to you in His Word what He desires for you to take as the next step of growth in your journey toward wise financial stewardship.

As you conclude a time of study, ask the Lord to seal to your heart and mind what you have learned so that you will never forget it. Ask Him to transform you more into the likeness of Christ Jesus—so that you might use all of your resources in a way that is pleasing to Christ.

The Depth of God's Word

Avoid the temptation of concluding at the end of your ten-week study that you have all the information you need to be a prosperous person. In all likelihood, you have only begun this journey. Continue to read God's Word. You'll see evidence and examples related to financial stewardship, prosperity, and God's blessings in virtually every story in the Bible. Continue to grow and to explore what God has to say to you about what it means to be blessed and to be a blessing.

Never stop exploring the riches of God's Word on any topic. I can guarantee you without reservation that as you remain faithful in reading God's Word on a daily basis, you'll have a much greater understanding a year from now about what it means to be whole and to be prosperous. Grow in your understanding of God's truth.

- *What new insights about finances and stewardship do you anticipate God may have for you personally and individually? Are there money-related needs in your life for which you need God's answer or supply? Is there something specific that you hope to gain from this study?*

  _____

  _____

- *In what areas have you struggled with money or stewardship in the past?*

  _____

  _____

- *How do you feel about prosperity? How do you feel about the word* stewardship? *How do you feel when you face the prospect of receiving a financial blessing? How do you feel when you face the prospect of giving?*

  _____

  _____

- *Do you feel challenged to grow in your understanding of financial stewardship as a means of becoming a more effective witness for Christ Jesus? In what ways? Are you ready to embark on that growth today?*

  _____

  _____

LESSON 2

THE PLACE OF MONEY IN YOUR LIFE

How much money can a Christian make and still be a Christian? How much money can a Christian have and still be spiritually minded? Is there an income level at which someone stops being obedient to God?

These questions, and others like them, often enter into conversations that I have with people about money and material wealth. Many people seem to believe that money and spirituality are incompatible. Some of this belief seems to have come from teachings related to two verses in the Bible. Let's take a look at them at the very beginning of our study about financial stewardship.

A Blessing on Poverty?

The first verse is a very familiar one. It's from the passage of Scripture that we call the Beatitudes:

Blessed are the poor in spirit,
For theirs is the kingdom of heaven (Matt. 5:3).

People seem to assume that because this passage uses the word *poor*, the Lord was talking about people who were living in financial poverty. They conclude that poverty is linked to spirituality. I've heard people say only somewhat in jest about their preachers, "We'll keep 'em poor, and God will keep 'em humble." These people have come to the position that being poor removes all concern or desire for material provision, and that once individuals have given up all hope of any prosperity, God can speak more clearly to them. Some even seem to conclude that all poor people make it to heaven and that no rich people do.

We know from a very practical, logical standpoint that this is not the case. Poor people don't stop being concerned about financial provision or cease desiring prosperity. If anything, they have a greater concern about meeting their material needs. Millions of people around the world awaken every morning with poverty foremost on their minds, and they spend long hours trying to eke out the barest of livings in their effort to stave off death, disease, oppression, and other horrible ravages of poverty. Poverty doesn't automatically make people more conscious of God or more spiritually minded.

Furthermore, God doesn't stop speaking to the rich. He speaks to any person who has a listening heart, regardless of the balance in the checkbook.

Perhaps the more important issue, however, is that this verse doesn't say what people have come to think it says. Jesus refers to the "poor in spirit," not the poor in finances. He is speaking about those who are humble, who have no pretense that they are beyond any need of God's forgiveness. People must be poor in spirit—in other words, have an attitude that they need God and are spiritually destitute without Him—before they will ever turn to God and receive His forgiveness and love.

To a great degree, our sense of having a lack of God in our lives draws us to want a relationship with God. And when we come to that point in our lives, we are in the best position possible to accept Jesus Christ as our Savior and to receive God's forgiveness in our lives. When we accept Jesus and open ourselves to God's forgiveness and love, we have entrance into eternal life and a permanent home in heaven. Ours is the kingdom of heaven, as Jesus taught.

Can a rich person be humble before God? Can a rich person feel a need for God? Can a rich person experience salvation and place all her trust in God? The answer is yes.

Can a poor person be too angry with God to seek His forgiveness? Can a poor person refuse to turn to God for forgiveness? Can a poor person reject God's offer of forgiveness and remain a sinner? Again, the answer is yes.

"But," some say, "there is a spirit of poverty, and those who have this spirit are more likely to turn to God." Yes, there is a spirit of poverty. It is a spirit that causes depression, dejection, and despair. It is a spirit that manifests itself in poor self-esteem, low levels of confidence and enthusiasm, and a lack of hope. It is a spirit that can result in such fear and anxiety that faith is crushed. A spirit of poverty exists, but it is not a spirit that automatically causes a person to turn to God. Having a spirit of poverty is not at all the same as being "poor in spirit."

Finally, I've met people who grew up poor but never seemed to think of themselves as poor. They were surrounded by people who loved them, believed in them, encouraged them in their faith, and held out the hope of a bright future to them. They look back on their financially meager childhoods and think of themselves as having been very rich in all the right things.

I've also met people who grew up in wealthy homes, but they are impoverished when it comes to love, hope, enthusiasm for the future, and self-image. They were given lots of material stuff, but not much love or attention. No, financial blessing doesn't automatically relate to the salvation of one's soul or a decision to follow in the footsteps of Jesus Christ. There is no inherent righteousness in poverty.

- *Have you ever been poor in spirit? How did you feel?*

_____

_____

- *Recall an instance in your past when you didn't have very much money. How did you feel?*

  _____

  _____

- *In what ways were these experiences and your feelings about them similar? Dissimilar?*

  _____

  _____

The Poor with Us

A second verse that is often used to support the idea that poverty is linked to spirituality is this: "The poor you have with you always" (John 12:8).

People have used this verse to conclude that God condones poverty. That is not what this verse says. There is no blessing attached with poverty, in this verse or any other verse. Jesus was pointing out to His disciples the reality of humankind as a whole, not God's desire for humankind. He was stating what is, not what God wishes.

Furthermore, we need to take this statement in the broader context of what was happening in the lives of Jesus and His disciples at that point. Jesus was in the house of Mary, Martha, and Lazarus, whom Jesus had recently raised from the dead. Jesus was having supper with them only a week before His crucifixion, and He knew His time on earth was short. The Bible tells us,

> Mary took a pound of very costly oil of spikenard, anointed the feet of Jesus, and wiped His feet with her hair. And the house was filled with the fragrance of the oil. But one of His disciples, Judas Iscariot, Simon's son, who would betray Him, said, "Why was this fragrant oil not sold for three hundred denarii and given to the poor?" This he said, not that he cared for the poor, but because he was a thief, and had the money box; and he used to take what was put in it.

But Jesus said, "Let her alone; she has kept this for the day of My burial. For the poor you have with you always, but Me you do not have always" (John 12:3–8).

Jesus' main point was not that the poor are always in our midst, but that Judas's priorities were sorely misplaced. Judas claimed to be thinking of what could be given to the poor when he was really concerned about having more money in the fund from which he was embezzling. Judas had no sensitivity toward what God was about to do in Jesus' life; he had no sensitivity toward the motive of Mary's heart. Jesus clearly and accurately read Judas's intentions and stated just as clearly that any gift given out of sacrificial love for the Lord is a worthy gift.

There is no honor bestowed upon poverty in this statement of Jesus.

- *How do you feel about poverty today? When you hear the word* prosperity, *how do you feel?*

_____

_____

What Is the Place of Money in Your Life?

Apart from linking poverty and spirituality, there are three positions that people tend to hold toward money and material gain.

1. Idolatry

For some people, money becomes central to their lives They worship money, which means that they devote most of their time, energy, and attention to its gain and use. They regard money as the key to having power and prestige.

"I'd never worship the idol of finance," you may say. But ask yourself these questions:

- How much time do I spend thinking about my material or financial life every day—my income, my bills, my past and upcoming purchases, my investments? In comparison, how much time do I spend in God's Word or meditating upon it?

- How much time do I spend working, shopping, or dealing with money in any given week? Be sure to include trips to the automatic teller machines and the bank, discussions with your spouse about budgets or spending plans and habits, and the time you spend paying bills and balancing your checking account. In comparison, how much time do I spend in prayer, reading my Bible, or participating in church-related activities and outreaches?

- Am I more likely to discuss with my family and friends a hot stock tip, the cost of an item, or a new business opportunity . . . or an insight I have into God's Word, the major truths of last Sunday's sermon, or a way in which the Holy Spirit helped me during the day? Into which conversation am I likely to put more energy, enthusiasm, or concern?

You may say that you trust God in every area of your life, but then you conduct business transactions, make purchases and investments, and enter into money-making opportunities without ever asking God's opinion or seeking God's wisdom.

An idol can be anything that you place above God in your heart and mind. It is anything that you trust more than you trust God. It is anything that you love more than God and the things of God.

When you leave God out of your financial life, you are in grave danger of making money your idol.

- *In your past experience, can you point to a time in which you will admit that money was an idol to you?*

_____

_____

- *In what ways are you feeling challenged today?*

_____

_____

The Bible has much to say about false idols. Remind yourself of these verses below. Apply them to your financial life.

What the Word Says	What the Word Says to Me
I am the LORD your God. . . . You shall have no other gods before Me (Ex. 20:2–3).	_____ _____ _____
Do you not know that the unrighteous will not inherit the kingdom of God? Do not be deceived. Neither . . . idolaters . . . nor extortioners will inherit the kingdom of God (1 Cor. 6:9–10).	_____ _____ _____ _____ _____ _____
Therefore, my beloved, flee from idolatry (1 Cor. 10:14).	_____ _____

2. Envy

A second position that people often have toward money is best stated as envy. Now, they aren't likely to admit they are envious. They are more likely to say, "I'm poor but honest." The assumption underlying that statement is that those who are rich aren't honest.

People who hold this position assume that those who have money must have gained it through illegal, immoral, or otherwise ungodly means. They suspect cheating to have been required at some point. Or they believe that the rich are rich because they are selfish and they refuse to give to the poor what "rightfully" belongs to the poor.

Why do people hold this position? Usually because they feel cheated in some way. They think that the rich have what they have, to at least some degree, because they have taken it from the person or people who don't have as much.

That is rarely the case.

Most people with great wealth in our nation have it because they have worked very hard, have invested their time and money very astutely, or have inherited their money (which means someone before them worked hard and invested time and money wisely).

Furthermore, the rich do not owe the poor anything that the poor are capable of earning for themselves.

Reread that statement very carefully. I don't want you to misunderstand what I am saying. We are called upon very clearly in the Bible to take care of the poor and to provide for the poor, but the poor are always assumed in the Scriptures to be those who are incapable of taking care of themselves. The poor are nearly always defined as widows and orphans—those who do not have a designated provider within a family structure. "The poor" is not a classification according to financial status—in other words, those who fall below the poverty line. "The poor" in the Bible is a classification according to a lack of provider, or a lack of an ability to meet needs. In plain, modern-day language, we are to help *those who have nobody else to help them*, which may very well include abandoned children, older people, desperately sick or injured people, or others who are alone and in dire need.

The Bible clearly states that able-bodied and capable people are to work and provide for their own needs. Furthermore, the Bible speaks very strongly against these things:

- Procrastination
- Laziness
- Slothfulness
- An unwillingness to become the maximum that God created a person to be

The Bible teaches that people have a responsibility for doing the utmost they can for themselves. And then after they have done all they know to do or are capable of doing, the community at large is to provide what still remains as a need. This provision is to come not only from the wealthy but also from all who have any excess in their lives.

At no place in the Scriptures do we find the Lord commanding us to take on freeloaders or to pay the entire bill for those who are capable of earning at least part of their way. The poor are given no right to expect the rich to pay any portion of the bills that they can pay for themselves. We are to help people improve their lot in life and to help them climb the economic ladder. But at no time does God command us to become the sole source of provision for lazy, unproductive, and willfully slothful people.

In the vast majority of cases, the wealthy people in our society provide jobs for the poor and create opportunities for the poor to be helped.

Now, it is not only the destitute and poor who can feel envious of the wealth of others. Envious people may very well have a great deal, but they don't have what they think they should have or what they think they deserve. Some people who have a great deal are sorely dissatisfied with their lot in life. They feel it unfair if someone else has more than they have.

- *How do you feel about people who have less than you have in terms of material possessions or wealth?*

  _____

  _____

- *How do you feel about people who have more than you have in terms of material possessions or wealth?*

  _____

  _____

In the Bible, people who are envious of the things that others have—and who believe that the things of others belong more rightfully to them than to the current owners—are called *covetous*.

Remind yourself of what God has to say about covetous people.

What the Word Says

What the Word Says to Me

You shall not covet your neighbor's house; you shall not covet your neighbor's wife, nor his male servant, nor his female servant, nor his ox, nor his donkey, nor anything that is your neighbor's (Ex. 20:17).

[Paul said,] "I have coveted no one's silver or gold or apparel. Yes, you yourselves know that these hands have provided for my necessities, and for those who were with me. I have shown you in every way, by laboring like this, that you must support the weak. And remember the words of the Lord Jesus, that He said, 'It is more blessed to give than to receive'" (Acts 20:33–35).

Let your conduct be without covetousness; be content with such things as you have. For He Himself has said, "I will never leave you nor forsake you." So we may boldly say:
"The LORD is my helper;
I will not fear.
What can man do to me?" (Heb. 13:5–6).

He who hates covetousness will
prolong his days (Prov. 28:16).

_____

_____

Greed. Both idolatry and envy are positions toward money that can easily result in greed. Greed is an insatiable desire for more. It is an attitude that is not limited to money and possessions, but is often related to money and material goods. People with great wealth, people with no wealth, and people of all economic levels in between are equally prone to greed, for greed is a state of the heart.

The greedy person says, "I deserve more than I have simply because I want more." Such a person rarely acknowledges she has responsibility for her current lot in life. She tends to blame others for the lack she feels.

At the core of greed are a refusal to take personal responsibility and a refusal to trust God. The greedy person does not truly believe that God will take care of him, that God loves him, or that God has blessed him. He tends to regard God as a stingy, unfair victimizer.

At the very bottom of her heart, the greedy person believes that if God truly loved her, God would give her everything she desires. The greedy person wants God to prove His love for her through a shower of material blessings. Two main problems exist, however: (1) the greedy person denies that God might express His love in any other terms than the material, and (2) there is no end to what the greedy heart desires.

The greedy person does not allow God to fill the void he feels in his heart with God's presence. He wants things to fill the void. Money and possessions—both tangible and intangible—can never fill that void; therefore, the voracious "hunger" associated with greed is never satisfied. The greedy person wants more, more, more, more of everything, that is, except God.

The Bible has much to say about the greedy person—none of it good.

What the Word Says

The desire of the lazy man kills
him,

What the Word Says to Me

_____

_____

For his hands refuse to labor.

He covets greedily all day long,

But the righteous gives and does

not spare (Prov. 21:25–26).

Their feet run to evil,

And they make haste to shed
blood.

Surely, in vain the net is spread

In the sight of any bird;

But they lie in wait for their own
blood,

They lurk secretly for their own
lives.

So are the ways of everyone who
is greedy for gain;

It takes away the life of its owners (Prov. 1:16–19).

He who is greedy for gain trou-
bles his own house (Prov. 15:27).

Do not conclude too quickly that you are free of all greed in your
life. To whatever degree you fail to trust God completely to meet
all your needs—spiritual, mental, emotional, physical, material,
relational—you are prone to greed.

3. Neutrality

The third position we can take toward money is this: money is
neutral. This is the position that I believe is wise to take. A
twenty-dollar bill can be used to buy a bottle of booze, which can
help lead to a ruined life, or to buy a Bible for a person who doesn't
know the Lord, which can help lead to eternal life. The twenty-
dollar bill, in and of itself, has no morality associated with it. In
other words, it's the attitude toward our money—and then what
we do with our money—that counts.

God is far more concerned about your attitudes and desires toward money than He is about your current bank statement. He is far more concerned about how you spend your money and allocate your resources than with your starting or ending balance.

Consider the verses below in the light of finances and your attitude toward money.

What the Word Says	What the Word Says to Me
As he thinks in his heart, so is he (Prov. 23:7).	_____
	_____
Do not be deceived, God is not mocked; for whatever a man sows, that he will also reap. For he who sows to his flesh will of the flesh reap corruption, but he who sows to the Spirit will of the Spirit reap everlasting life. And let us not grow weary while doing good, for in due season we shall reap if we do not lose heart. Therefore, as we have opportunity, let us do good to all, especially to those who are of the household of faith (Gal. 6:7–10).	_____
	_____
	_____
	_____
	_____
	_____
	_____
	_____
	_____
	_____
	_____

- *What new insights do you have into poverty and prosperity?*

  _____

- *In what ways are you feeling challenged today?*

  _____

  _____

LESSON 3

MONEY AND YOUR FAITH

There is a strong correlation between money, which includes all of your material wealth and your attitude toward possessions, and your faith, or your spiritual life. The way you handle money indicates a great deal about your relationship with God.

Godliness has a dimension of concern and care about the handling of the material world, including stewardship of nature. Just as God is concerned about His material creation, so you are to be concerned about the material world. For the godly, however, the foremost concern in life is to be placed on spiritual growth and development.

The ungodly are careless with the material and natural world, although they spend most of their time thinking about ways to use it for purposes of making money. They have virtually no concern for nourishing their spiritual nature.

In Revelation 18:9–19 we see that a sign of the end times is an overemphasis on riches and a total preoccupation with material goods. It is a graphic manifestation of how the ungodly have run their course and have spent their all on material pursuits:

> The kings of the earth who committed fornication and lived luxuriously with [the queen of Babylon] will weep and lament for her, when they see the smoke of her burning,

standing at a distance for fear of her torment, saying, "Alas, alas, that great city Babylon, that mighty city! For in one hour your judgment has come." And the merchants of the earth will weep and mourn over her, for no one buys their merchandise anymore: merchandise of gold and silver, precious stones and pearls, fine linen and purple, silk and scarlet, every kind of citron wood, every kind of object of ivory, every kind of object of most precious wood, bronze, iron, and marble; and cinnamon and incense, fragrant oil and frankincense, wine and oil, fine flour and wheat, cattle and sheep, horses and chariots, and bodies and souls of men. The fruit that your soul longed for has gone from you, and all the things which are rich and splendid have gone from you, and you shall find them no more at all. The merchants of these things, who became rich by her, will stand at a distance for fear of her torment, weeping and wailing, and saying, "Alas, alas, that great city that was clothed in fine linen, purple, and scarlet, and adorned with gold and precious stones and pearls! For in one hour such great riches came to nothing." Every shipmaster, all who travel by ship, sailors, and as many as trade on the sea, stood at a distance and cried out when they saw the smoke of her burning, saying, "What is like this great city?" They threw dust on their heads and cried out, weeping and wailing, and saying, "Alas, alas, that great city, in which all who had ships on the sea became rich by her wealth! For in one hour she is made desolate."

What a picture we have in this passage! The leaders, the merchants, the sailors, and the traders are all devastated at their loss of wealth. There is no mention of the state of their souls. They have completely sacrificed their faith at the altar of wealth. Their entire pursuit in life has turned to a pursuit of material gain; there is no mention of spiritual gain or loss. They are ungodly to their core.

- *In your experience, have you or someone you have known fallen into this trap of pursuing material gain to the detriment of your spiritual life?*

• *How do you feel as you read this passage from Revelation?*

Let me be very clear on this point: a concern about material gain is not in itself ungodly. Rather, a concern for material wealth that chokes out and rules over a concern for one's spiritual gain and one's mental and emotional and family health is ungodly. A life out of balance is a life destined for failure, not success.

The fact that God desires for us to register a balanced concern for material gain is found throughout the Scriptures. The Lord desires for us to grow in every area of our lives—to be growing spiritually, physically, mentally, emotionally, in friendships and family ties, and in material sustenance, always in balance, but always growing. We are to invest our many abilities, skills, and assets wisely so that growth is possible. When we completely abandon our potential, refusing to do anything with the many gifts God has given us, God is displeased. He is not displeased that we gain wealth. He is displeased when we gain wealth at the expense of all other areas of our lives.

Jesus taught this principle in one of His most famous parables:

For the kingdom of heaven is like a man traveling to a far country, who called his own servants and delivered his goods to them. And to one he gave five talents, to another two, and to another one, to each according to his own ability; and immediately he went on a journey. Then he who had received the five talents went and traded with them, and made another five talents. And likewise he who had received two gained two more also. But he who had received one went and dug in the ground, and hid his lord's money. After a long time the lord of those servants came and settled accounts with them. So he who had received five talents came and brought five other talents, saying,

"Lord, you delivered to me five talents; look, I have gained five more talents besides them." His lord said to him, "Well done, good and faithful servant; you were faithful over a few things, I will make you ruler over many things. Enter into the joy of your lord." He also who had received two talents came and said, "Lord, you delivered to me two talents; look, I have gained two more talents besides them." His lord said to him, "Well done, good and faithful servant; you have been faithful over a few things, I will make you ruler over many things. Enter into the joy of your lord." Then he who had received the one talent came and said, "Lord, I knew you to be a hard man, reaping where you have not sown, and gathering where you have not scattered seed. And I was afraid, and went and hid your talent in the ground. Look, there you have what is yours." But his lord answered and said to him, "You wicked and lazy servant, you knew that I reap where I have not sown, and gather where I have not scattered seed. So you ought to have deposited my money with the bankers, and at my coming I would have received back my own with interest. Therefore take the talent from him, and give it to him who has ten talents. For to everyone who has, more will be given, and he will have abundance; but from him who does not have, even what he has will be taken away. And cast the unprofitable servant into the outer darkness. There will be weeping and gnashing of teeth" (Matt. 25:14–30).

- *In your experience, have you enjoyed benefit from talents well invested? Have you ever been like the servant who buried this talent and did nothing with it? What were the results in each case?*

- *How did you feel when you invested your talents or gave of yourself? How did you feel when you ignored or denied investing your potential or giving your best?*

- *How did you feel when you received a blessing from the Lord? How did you feel when you received chastisement from the Lord?*

Points from the Parable

I want you to notice several things from this parable that Jesus taught.

First, all of the initial talents given are from the lord. He gave the talents freely to his servants and intended for them to use them and be blessed in the process.

Everything you have is a gift from God to you. He expects you to use what you have been given and, as you use it, to be blessed.

If you are sitting back today and refusing to use some or all of the talents that God has given to you—whether out of fear, laziness, or disinterest—you are greatly limiting God's blessing in your life. Furthermore, you are cutting short your joy in life. And ultimately, you are denying yourself a closer relationship with God.

Notice the repeated phrase, "Enter into the joy of your lord." Jesus was teaching that people who risk their potential and invest what they have are not only subject to tangible reward—to rule over even more—but they are going to experience the pleasure of the Lord. God delights in people who give of themselves and who are willing to trust Him to honor their efforts. Such people are pleasing to God; they give Him joy, and they, in turn, share in that joy. Their relationship with God is an exhilarating, enthusiastic, loving, joyful one!

- *Are you experiencing a joyful relationship with the Lord? What new insights do you have regarding "the joy of your Lord"?*

_____

_____

Second, each of the servants was given a different amount of talents. One servant was given five talents, another two talents, and another one talent. Jesus said that was "according to his own ability." There are people who are gifted or blessed in unique ways. They have greater capacities for learning, for receiving, for giving, than other people have.

Some people consider this discouraging news. They don't feel this is fair. But this is life. God knew from the outset that certain people would be more ambitious than others—they would invest themselves more fully, work harder, use their talents more efficiently—and He knew that the end result would be a society in which some people seemed to have acquired everything and others nothing. That was one of the reasons, I believe, that God instituted the year of Jubilee for the children of Israel. Every fifty years, all debts were to be canceled, and those who had submitted themselves to slavery to pay their debts were to be set free. The playing field was made more level so that the nation as a whole could remain in balance.

You could wipe away the financial slates of every person in our nation today, and within a few years, you would again have wealthy people and poor people. This would not be solely because some are five-talent and two-talent people and others are one-talent people. Some people are willing to invest themselves—to give of who they are and what they have—and others are not. Some five-talent people don't use their talents. Some two-talent people don't give of themselves or develop their potential. Some one-talent people are doing all they can and giving all they can. The issue is not the amount of talents people have been given, but what they are doing with their talents.

Jesus taught,

> He who is faithful in what is least is faithful also in much;
> and he who is unjust in what is least is unjust also in much.

Therefore if you have not been faithful in the unrighteous mammon, who will commit to your trust the true riches? And if you have not been faithful in what is another man's, who will give you what is your own? (Luke 16:10–12).

You must never lose sight of the fact that in this story every servant was given something. You have a gift from God. You have one or more spiritual gifts, mental capabilities, physical attributes, emotional propensities, material possessions, and natural talents. The fact that you have them is not what matters. The important thing is this: What are you doing with what you have been given?

- *In your life experience, what have you come to recognize as your foremost talents in each of these areas:*
  Spiritual gifts?

_____

_____

Physical abilities?

_____

_____

Mental capabilities?

_____

_____

Emotional temperament?

_____

_____

Material possessions?

_____

_____

Other natural talents?

_____

_____

• *In what ways are you being challenged today regarding their use?*

_____

_____

Third, the servant who refused to risk investing his one talent did so out of fear. Fear is the number one obstacle that keeps people from giving of themselves or taking the risks necessary to realize their potential. These fears are not rooted in an external, outer reality as much as they are fears of the mind and heart:

• A fear of failure
• A fear of disappointment—either of disappointing others or disappointing ourselves
• A fear of what others will say about us—a fear of losing face or diminishing our reputation
• A fear of loss and of being a lesser person

The servant in Jesus' parable said that he was afraid of his master's displeasure. Some people are afraid that God will punish them for making a mistake, so they refuse to take any risks with their faith.

Fear doesn't keep us from failure. Fear causes failure. The lord in this parable punished the unprofitable servant not for failing to succeed, but for failing to try! That's a very important point related to faith.

God does not require that we be successful. He does not punish us for failing to succeed. But He is very disappointed when we fail to give our best and fail to make the attempt.

When a person refuses to take a risk because he is fearful—whether a risk in giving his money, developing a natural talent, or pursuing a new learning challenge—that person is saying these things about his relationship with God:

- "I don't trust God to help me accomplish this or direct me wisely so that I can succeed."
- "I don't trust God to reward my effort, only punish my failure."

Can you see how integral faith in God is to the management of your material goods and your many talents? Either you trust God to help you, teach you, guide you, and lead you to the place where He will reward you, or you don't. Either you believe God is on your side and desires to help you fulfill your God-given potential and reap the blessings He has prepared for you, or you believe that God is against you and is waiting in the shadows to find an excuse to destroy you, undermine you, or defeat you.

- *How do you feel about God's desires for you today?*

_____

_____

Ultimately, you must come to the position where you will admit to yourself and to God: "I trust You enough to obey Your Word, do Your will, give my best, use my talents, commit myself to You completely, and operate in financial stewardship the way You have prescribed," or "I don't trust You, and therefore, I will live my life according to my own wits and will." Either you trust God with all of your life, or you don't.

- *What new insights do you have into this parable that Jesus taught about the talents?*

_____

_____

Prosperity vs. Riches

In our discussion of money and faith, we need to remind ourselves that prosperity and riches are two different things. The difference is summarized below:

Prosperity	Riches
having all you need and the capacity to enjoy it	the accumulation of wealth (money and goods)
being fruitful	
growing	
all areas of life in balance	
specific to God's plan for you	

Prosperity includes material gain but is not limited to it. It includes balanced growth and multiplication in all areas of life.

The accumulation of wealth is something that you can do without God. You can engage in the various means of acquiring worldly goods and leave God out of the process. You only need to look around at our world today to see that many people are doing just this.

But you cannot be prosperous without God. You cannot have a fully balanced, fruitful, and joyful life without God. To be truly prosperous, you must be spiritually prosperous—your faith and relationship with God must be growing and fruitful. That can't happen apart from God.

Both rich people and poor people are miserable without God. But prosperous people—whether they start out with five talents or one talent—are joyful, productive, and enthusiastic people. Why? Because prosperous people are growing. They have a sense of accomplishment. They are bearing good fruit. They have balanced lives and therefore have a sense of fulfillment and satisfaction.

Both rich people and poor people are prone to jealousy of the wealth of others because they are never satisfied until they have all the wealth they can envision or all the wealth they think they need. They regard others who have more than they have as having something that belongs, or will belong, rightfully to them. In comparison, prosperous people rejoice at the prosperity of others.

They are delighted when others are fruitful and growing because they know there is no limit to what God can do in a person's life.

Rich people trust only themselves.

Prosperous people trust God to show them the ways to be fruitful, to grow, to stay balanced, and to know and do God's will.

It takes no faith in God to become rich. It takes faith in God to become prosperous.

What the Word Says	What the Word Says to Me
Beloved, I pray that you may prosper in all things and be in health, just as your soul prospers. For I rejoiced greatly when brethren came and testified of the truth that is in you, just as you walk in the truth. I have no greater joy than to hear that my children walk in truth (3 John 2–4).	
He who trusts in his riches will fall, But the righteous will flourish like foliage (Prov. 11:28).	
He who heeds the word wisely will find good, And whoever trusts in the LORD, happy is he (Prov. 16:20).	
You will keep him in perfect peace, Whose mind is stayed on You, Because he trusts in You. Trust in the LORD forever,	

For in YAH, the LORD, is ever- _____
lasting strength (Isa. 26:3–4). _____

Finally, prosperity has a lasting, eternal quality. Riches can be wiped away in a day—or in an hour as we read from Revelation earlier in this lesson. Prosperity lasts. Even during times of temporary loss or lack, even during slow times or lulls in one area of life, the person who desires God's prosperity and is living according to God's principles for prosperity has a deep, abiding sense of the Lord's presence, provision, and pleasure.

The person who desires to be prosperous lives in such a way that the promises of God are available to him. The person who seeks only riches is someone to whom the fullness of God's promises does not apply.

The person who strives to be rich limits himself to living by the "flesh," which is a scriptural way of saying that a person is limiting himself solely to his capabilities and capacities as a human being. The person who pursues prosperity avails herself of God's ability to bless her. She is not limited to what she can do as a person. She is connecting her life to the unlimited God, therefore, there is no limit to the amount of growth and blessing that she might enjoy.

The servants in the parable doubled their investments, but when their lord rewarded them, he said he would make them rulers over "many things." The message is that there is no end to God's ability to bless people or to cause them to be filled with His goodness.

The prophet Jeremiah painted a vivid picture of this:

> *Thus says the LORD:*
> *"Cursed is the man who trusts in man*
> *And makes flesh his strength,*
> *Whose heart departs from the LORD.*
> *For he shall be like a shrub in the desert,*
> *And shall not see when good comes,*
> *But shall inhabit the parched places in the wilderness,*
> *In a salt land which is not inhabited.*

Blessed is the man who trusts in the LORD,
And whose hope is the LORD,
For he shall be like a tree planted by the waters,
Which spreads out its roots by the river,
And will not fear when heat comes;
But its leaf will be green,
And will not be anxious in the year of drought,
Nor will cease from yielding fruit" (Jer. 17:5–8).

God's desire for you is prosperity. He desires that you be a whole person, balanced and growing and fruitful and fulfilling His plan and purpose for your life. You must ask yourself: What is my desire? How am I acting on it?

- *What new insights do you have into the nature of prosperity and poverty?*

  _____

  _____

- *What new insights do you have into the relationship between your material life and your spiritual life?*

  _____

  _____

- *In what ways are you being challenged by God today?*

  _____

  _____

LESSON 4

THE SOURCE OF YOUR PROSPERITY

The Bible is filled from cover to cover with the goodness of God. Our heavenly Father is always giving, always loving, always generous toward His children. In Genesis, He gives the man and woman He makes a perfect Garden of Eden. In Revelation, we read about our ultimate home, a perfect and eternal heaven. In all the books in between, we read how God delighted in blessing His people. At the outset of the New Testament, we read how God sent His Son, Jesus Christ, as His ultimate gift of blessing to us.

God is the Source of all you need. He is the Author of the whole-life, eternal-life prosperity plan. The sovereignty of God over all material wealth is stated clearly in 1 Chronicles 29:10–14. These words of King David also reflect the attitude we should have toward God's provision:

> Therefore David blessed the LORD before all the assembly; and David said:
> "Blessed are You, LORD God of Israel, our Father, forever and ever.
> Yours, O LORD, is the greatness,
> The power and the glory,
> The victory and the majesty;
> For all that is in heaven and in earth is Yours;

> *Yours is the kingdom, O LORD,*
> *And You are exalted as head over all.*
> *Both riches and honor come from You,*
> *And You reign over all.*
> *In Your hand is power and might;*
> *In Your hand it is to make great*
> *And to give strength to all.*
> *Now therefore, our God,*
> *We thank You*
> *And praise Your glorious name.*
> *But who am I, and who are my people,*
> *That we should be able to offer so willingly as this?*
> *For all things come from You,*
> *And of Your own we have given You."*

If we were to summarize David's statement in three short sentences, we would likely say:

1. The Lord is the owner of everything.

2. The Lord gives generously to His people.

3. We do well to give Him thanks and praise for what He has given us.

Jesus certainly held to this same conclusion when He taught His disciples to conclude their times of prayer by saying, "For Yours is the kingdom and the power and the glory forever. Amen" (Matt. 6:13). God owns everything, has all authority to dispense with it as He chooses, and is worthy of all praise for what He does forever. And let it be so!

When David reflected about going up to the house of the LORD in Jerusalem, he sang,

> *Pray for the peace of Jerusalem:*
> *"May they prosper who love you.*
> *Peace be within your walls,*
> *Prosperity within your palaces" (Ps. 122:6–7).*

He gave us a prayer that we can pray for all Christians, a prayer that is totally in line with God's will for His people.

The Scriptures are filled with verses that tell us of God's goodness, His inexhaustible resources, and His desire to prosper His people. God's desire for you is prosperity—that you might have all you need and the capacity to enjoy it.

As you read the verses below, apply them to your life.

What the Word Says

What the Word Says to Me

Hear me, O Judah and you inhabitants of Jerusalem: Believe in the LORD your God, and you shall be established; believe His prophets, and you shall prosper (2 Chron. 20:20).

_____

Every good gift and every perfect gift is from above, and comes down from the Father of lights, with whom there is no variation or shadow of turning (James 1:17).

_____

My God shall supply all your need according to His riches in glory by Christ Jesus (Phil. 4:19).

_____

Oh, taste and see that the LORD is good;
Blessed is the man who trusts in Him!
Oh, fear the LORD, you His saints!
There is no want to those who fear Him.
The young lions lack and suffer hunger;

_____

But those who seek the LORD
shall not lack any good thing (Ps.
34:8–10).

When you limit yourself to your own ability and resources, you find that you run out of both ability and resources very quickly. When you focus your faith on what God can do for you, you confront an infinite supply that cannot be measured and therefore cannot be depleted. God's resources are 100 percent inflation-proof, depression-proof, and recession-proof.

The very nature of God gives you assurance of His abundant provision:

- Omniscient—God knows your need. He knows it even better than you do and before you do.
- Omnipotent—God has all power to supply to you what you need.
- Omnipresent—God is at work even now to meet your needs.

Not only do you have the character of God as your assurance that He is going to provide for you, but you also have testimony of God's past performance in providing for His people. The Scriptures repeatedly point to Him as a faithful Source:

- He made a way for His people to cross the Red Sea and be delivered from their enemies.
- He provided manna for the people to eat in the wilderness.
- He caused water to gush forth from a rock to quench His people's thirst.
- He gave His commandments to the people when they were without moral fiber.
- He healed His people when they were struck by poisonous snakes.

His provision for His people was complete, in every area of their lives.

- *In your past experience, can you identify several instances in which God truly manifested Himself to you as the Source of what you needed?*

  _____

  _____

- *As you reflect on the goodness of God, what new insights do you have into His desire to bring you into prosperity?*

  _____

  _____

God's Provision for All Your Need

In Philippians 4:19, God promises to supply all your need. You have very specific needs—emotional, physical, material, mental, and spiritual. All your needs must be met if you are to carry out the complete life plan God has ordained for you.

When you look at need, you must not compare yourself to others. Another person may have a different level of need because God has asked that person to do something that requires more resources of one type or another. You can be assured that God will always meet all of your needs.

Jesus spoke of God's promise to supply all your needs:

Therefore I say to you, do not worry about your life, what you will eat or what you will drink; nor about your body, what you will put on. Is not life more than food and the body more than clothing? Look at the birds of the air, for they neither sow nor reap nor gather into barns; yet your heavenly Father feeds them. Are you not of more value than they? Which of you by worrying can add one cubit to his stature? So why do you worry about clothing? Consider the lilies of the field, how they grow: they neither toil nor spin;

and yet I say to you that even Solomon in all his glory was not arrayed like one of these. Now if God so clothes the grass of the field, which today is, and tomorrow is thrown into the oven, will He not much more clothe you, O you of little faith? Therefore do not worry, saying, "What shall we eat?" or "What shall we drink?" or "What shall we wear?" For after all these things the Gentiles seek. For your heavenly Father knows that you need all these things. But seek first the kingdom of God and His righteousness, and all these things shall be added to you (Matt. 6:25–33).

Note that the Lord encourages you to seek first the things that are spiritual—the things that pertain to the kingdom of God and His righteousness. When you do that, the Lord adds everything else to your life. He gives you a total provision for a whole life. That's prosperity!

- *What new insights do you have into this teaching of Jesus from Matthew 6?*

  _____

  _____

- *How do you feel about God's being the Source of all your needs?*

  _____

  _____

I've met a number of people who have been honest enough to confess to me that they believe God is the Source of all things and that they believe God supplies abundantly for His people, but they have difficulty believing that God will provide for *them* individually and personally. They believe in the general principle and the broad truth that God takes care of His people, but they admit to doubts and questions about whether God will provide what they need.

Let's turn our attention to some areas that are related to this broader concern about whether God will meet personal needs.

Needs and Desires

First is the issue of needs versus desires.

A *need* is something that you must have in order to stay alive and to carry out God's will for your life. Unless your needs are met, you are unable to survive or fulfill the destiny God has ordained for you.

A *desire* is something that might be considered a pleasantry or a nicety. It's fun to have—enjoyable, satisfying, delightful.

Some people seem to believe that God provides only for our bare-essential needs. They question whether what they are requesting is truly a need, believing that if they ask for anything they desire but don't need, God will not grant it.

Does God meet only needs? No. That isn't the message of the Bible. God's provision for us is one of abundance. Jesus taught,

> The thief [the devil] does not come except to steal, and to kill, and to destroy. I have come that they may have life, and that they may have it more abundantly (John 10:10).

> Give, and it will be given to you: good measure, pressed down, shaken together, and running over will be put into your bosom (Luke 6:38).

God's desire for you is abundance—a pressed-down, shaken-together, and running-over prosperity. Don't be afraid to ask God for what you desire as well as what you need.

As a parent and a grandfather, I take great joy in giving things to my children and grandchildren. It isn't a matter of whether they need these things. I certainly see to it first and foremost that their basic needs are met. But I have joy in giving them things that are beyond their needs—in giving them the desires of their hearts. The heavenly Father has this same generosity of spirit toward you. He is not a stingy, cheap, or begrudging God.

God's only constraints regarding the desires of your heart are that they do not keep you from fulfilling His plan and purpose for you on the earth, and that they are things that will benefit you and not cause you harm.

Repeated Requests

Some people believe that God will not supply their needs, much less grant their desires, unless they meet certain requirements, one of which seems to be that they ask God repeatedly and frequently for what they need.

There is no need to plead or beg God for what you need. If that was the case, God would be no better than a miserly human being! God knows what you need. He already desires to meet your needs before you ask Him. So do ask, but don't feel you must ask repeatedly.

Preconditions

God asks certain things of you in order for you to be in a position to receive His generosity. I believe these commandments of God are intended to keep you looking to God so that you are fully capable of receiving from Him and then wisely using the abundance that He pours out on you. Obedience to God's plan keeps you disciplined.

1. God asks us to keep His commandments. Deuteronomy 28 is a wonderful example of this. The entire chapter will help you understand God's provision, but let me focus on just this one passage:

> If you diligently obey the voice of the LORD your God, to observe carefully all His commandments which I command you today, that the LORD your God will set you high above all nations of the earth. And all these blessings shall come upon you and overtake you, because you obey the voice of the LORD your God. . . . The LORD will grant you plenty of goods, in the fruit of your body, in the increase of your livestock, and in the produce of your ground, in the land of which the LORD swore to your fathers to give you. The LORD will open to you His good treasure, the heavens, to give the rain to your land in its season, and to bless all the work of your hand. You shall lend to many nations, but you shall not borrow. And the LORD will make you the head and not the tail; you shall be above only, and not be beneath, if you heed the commandments of the LORD your

God, which I command you today, and are careful to observe them. So you shall not turn aside from any of the words which I command you this day, to the right or the left, to go after other gods to serve them (Deut. 28:1–2, 11–14).

Note these words and phrases in the passage: "plenty of goods," "increase," "good treasure," "bless," and "head and not the tail." Note also that God's children are to have enough to lend to others, and that they will have no necessity to borrow. When you keep God's commandments and live according to His principles, you are in a position to enjoy this kind of prosperity.

2. *God also requires that you be generous and giving to others.* Note the balance in 1 Timothy 6:17–19:

Command those who are rich in this present age not to be haughty, nor to trust in uncertain riches but in the living God, who gives us richly all things to enjoy. Let them do good, that they be rich in good works, ready to give, willing to share, storing up for themselves a good foundation for the time to come, that they may lay hold on eternal life.

God trusts the generous person with more. He knows you will use what He gives you to bless others. And still, you will never suffer a deficit or loss because you will always be receiving an overflowing supply in return!

3. *God requires that you believe in Him and His Word.* If you don't believe God is going to supply all your need or grant you the desire of your heart, you aren't going to be looking for that supply or that desired object, person, or circumstance to arrive. In other words, you won't be ready for your blessing when it shows up. Refer back to 2 Chronicles 20:20. Believing that God will meet your needs and grant your desires is an important prerequisite to having your needs met and your desires granted.

If you are having difficulty believing that God will meet your personal needs, ask God to help you believe. Ask the Lord to help you with your attitude and to help you to trust Him more. That is a cry from the heart that God delights in answering. God longs to hear His people express their dependency on Him and to ask Him for help in trusting Him more.

Other Preconditions?

There is *no* precondition for you to have achieved sainthood for God before God will bless you. There is *no* precondition for certain rituals to be completed or for a certain number of hours to have been spent in prayer and fasting for a need to be answered. There is *no* checklist or point system that God uses in meting out rewards to His people. God desires that you trust Him to meet your needs, and trust is a matter of faith, not works. God desires that you give of what you have to bless others, and again, this is a matter of your trusting God, not a matter of working your way into a position to deserve rewards.

God's provision for you is out of His heart. It is motivated entirely by His unending love for you. It is not anything that you deserve or accomplish.

When you believe in God, keep His commandments, and begin to act with generosity toward others, you are in a position to receive from God more fully and more beneficially. God, however, is always in a position to give. He never moves from that position.

- *Have you ever received an extravagant gift from God?*

  _____

  _____

- *How do you feel about God's desire to give you an abundant life?*

  _____

  _____

- *In what ways are you feeling challenged today with regard to: the keeping of God's commandments?*

  _____

  _____

  the need to be generous toward others?

_____

_____

the need to believe that God will meet your needs?

_____

_____

A Uniform or Tailored Supply?

Some people erroneously believe that God supplies needs and grants desires uniformly—one provision fits all. That isn't the case. God's supply is always tailored to suit your specific, personal need. Sometimes you don't even know what that need involves. You may see only part of the need or even think your need lies in one area when it really lies in another area. God always supplies the true need.

Furthermore, God always supplies your need in the fullness of His timing. He gives what you need so that you might glorify Him and fulfill His purposes in the particular circumstance or season of life in which you find yourself.

The apostle Paul truly thought that his need was for the Lord to remove the "thorn in the flesh" that he experienced. Three times he prayed for the Lord to meet that need. God met Paul's need, but not in the way Paul envisioned. He made it clear to Paul that Paul really needed an awareness of God's grace that was capable of matching any need Paul might have. (See 2 Cor. 12:7–9.)

God's schedule and timetable don't always match yours, but let me assure you, God is never late in meeting your need.

Furthermore, God doesn't react to need. He knows your upcoming need and He has already prepared a provision to meet it. I experienced this in my life in a profound way prior to moving to Atlanta some twenty years ago. I received a sizable gift that was designated for my personal use, and as I prayed about what the Lord might want me to do with that gift, the Lord revealed that I should hold on to it for a while; His purposes would be revealed in His timing.

Four months later, the Lord directed me to move to Atlanta from Florida. The position in Atlanta did not have a parsonage associated with it, so for the first time in my ministry, I was required to buy a home. The amount I had been given four months previously was within one hundred dollars of the total down payment required for me to buy our first house.

What God gives to you He may not give to another person and vice versa. What God gives to you at one time in your life or in one season of your life may not be what God gives to you in another season. The children of Israel knew this in the gathering of manna. They were to gather just enough for the day; any excess spoiled. But on the day before the Sabbath, they were to gather two portions. The excess did not spoil, and they had a sufficient supply for two days. No manna was provided on the Sabbath day. So, too, with God's provision to you. Sometimes He meets the daily need only; at other times He gives you excess to use according to His purposes and plan. At times He calls upon you to rest in Him and to use past provision to meet your current need. (See Ex. 16:15–30.)

- *Have you had experiences in which God met your need, although He worked in a way you hadn't anticipated—perhaps meeting a deeper need or a need you hadn't realized you had?*

_____

- *Can you think of an experience you had of receiving God's provision with unusual or unexpected timing?*

_____

_____

Your Inability and God's Ability

You may find it useful to develop a little chart to remind yourself of God's all-sufficiency in meeting your needs and God's loving generosity in granting your desires.

Add to this list as you read God's Word regularly on your own.

My Ability to Supply My Needs	God's Ability and Desire to Supply My Needs
finite and limited	inexhaustible, infinite, unlimited
inadequate	totally adequate
disappears in famine	exists in famine
a constant battle against loss and diminishment	a constant provision in spite of generous giving

Above all, God desires to bless you with an abundance of spiritual gifts. God has "blessed [you] with every spiritual blessing" (Eph. 1:3). Come to your heavenly Father desiring the blessings as your first priority. Come to Him as a child He loves. Focus your faith on His love and His desire for you to have everything you need in this life and in the life to come.

Can you dip the ocean dry with a thimble?

Can your need—the thickness of a postage stamp—be compared to the mountain range of His supply?

No, you can never deplete the Source of your prosperity. You can only fail to come to Him and receive all that He has for you.

- *What new insights do you have into the nature of God-given prosperity?*

  _____

  _____

- *In what ways are you feeling challenged today?*

  _____

  _____

LESSON 5

THE ROLE OF WORK

If you want greater prosperity in your life, I believe there are two main things you need to do:

First, ask God to enlarge your faith. Your receiving of His blessing is directly related to your ability to believe God, to listen to His directives, and to act upon what He says to do.

Second, ask God to enlarge your usefulness—your capacity and ability to work.

More work?

Most people don't equate greater prosperity with greater work. As a society, we tend to want more money and less work. That, however, is not a scriptural principle. Work is God's divine plan to prosper us.

* *How do you feel about work?*

_____

_____

God's Plan for Work

God commands that we work. Even in giving Adam and Eve a perfect garden to call their home, God required them to "subdue" the earth—to dress and keep the garden, to have dominion over the other creatures, and to gather from creation the food they needed. God created Adam and Eve to participate fully in the ongoing management of His creation, and that required on their part exertion of effort and completion of tasks. Work is a part of our identity as human beings.

Proverbs 13:11 tells us plainly,

> *Wealth gained by dishonesty will be diminished,*
> *But he who gathers by labor will increase.*

God commends our labor. He chastises those who don't work.

One of the most quoted passages of the Bible is Proverbs 31:10–31, a passage about the "virtuous wife." This woman is held out as a model to follow. Note how many of the attributes ascribed to her relate to work. I invite you to underline all the passages that are about work—including volunteer or charitable work and work on behalf of others in her family—or about the wise management of resources.

> *Her worth is far above rubies.*
> *The heart of her husband safely trusts her;*
> *So he will have no lack of gain.*
> *She does him good and not evil*
> *All the days of her life.*
> *She seeks wool and flax,*
> *And willingly works with her hands.*
> *She is like the merchant ships,*
> *She brings her food from afar.*
> *She also rises while it is yet night,*
> *And provides food for her household,*
> *And a portion for her maidservants.*
> *She considers a field and buys it;*
> *From her profits she plants a vineyard.*
> *She girds herself with strength,*
> *And strengthens her arms.*
> *She perceives that her merchandise is good,*
> *And her lamp does not go out by night.*

She stretches out her hands to the distaff,
And her hand holds the spindle.
She extends her hand to the poor,
Yes, she reaches out her hands to the needy.
She is not afraid of snow for her household,
For all her household is clothed with scarlet.
She makes tapestry for herself;
Her clothing is fine linen and purple.
Her husband is known in the gates,
When he sits among the elders of the land.
She makes linen garments and sells them,
And supplies sashes for the merchants.
Strength and honor are her clothing;
She shall rejoice in time to come.
She opens her mouth with wisdom,
And on her tongue is the law of kindness.
She watches over the ways of her household;
And does not eat the bread of idleness.
Her children rise up and call her blessed;
Her husband also, and he praises her:
"Many daughters have done well,
But you excel them all."
Charm is deceitful and beauty is passing,
But a woman who fears the LORD, she shall be praised.
Give her of the fruit of her hands,
And let her own works praise her in the gates.

- *How do you feel about this description of a virtuous person?*

_____

_____

- *What new insights do you have into the nature of work?*

_____

_____

Some people think that if they just believe hard enough in God's ability to meet their needs, they will not have to work to provide for their sustenance. Some of the believers in the early church at

Thessalonica were like that. They were so intent on believing in the Lord's soon return that they spent their days going from house to house to stir up others in their belief. Paul had strong words for them and for any person today who is lazy or who mooches off others.

Paul had a strong tradition in his life of working for his keep as a tent maker (or leather worker). He did this as an example to any person who might think that a person engaged in ministry activities had a right to be lazy or escape putting forth any real effort. In God's eyes, all people need to employ all of their talents to the best of their ability and with a maximum amount of energy.

What the Word Says

We urge you, brethren, that you increase more and more; that you also aspire to lead a quiet life, to mind your own business, and to work with your own hands, as we commanded you, that you may walk properly toward those who are outside, and that you may lack nothing (1 Thess. 4:10–12).

For you yourselves know how you ought to follow us, for we were not disorderly among you; nor did we eat anyone's bread free of charge, but worked with labor and toil night and day, that we might not be a burden to any of you, not because we do not have authority, but to make our-

What the Word Says to Me

_____
_____
_____
_____
_____
_____
_____
_____
_____
_____

_____
_____
_____
_____
_____
_____
_____
_____
_____

selves an example of how you
should follow us. For even when
we were with you, we com-
manded you this: If anyone will
not work, neither shall he eat.
For we hear that there are some
who walk among you in a disorderly manner, not working at all,
but are busybodies. Now those
who are such we command and
exhort through our Lord Jesus
Christ that they work in quiet-
ness and eat their own bread (2
Thess. 3:7–12).

God requires that we work, and simultaneously, He leads others
to compensate us for our work. In 1 Thessalonians 4:10–12 above,
note that Paul speaks to the Thessalonians because he desires that
they "increase more and more." The virtuous woman of Proverbs
31 is to be praised and to receive rewards.

A marvelous example of compensation for good work is found
in the life of Joseph, the eleventh son of Jacob. Joseph was taken
by Ishmaelites down into Egypt, where an officer of Pharaoh
named Potiphar bought him as a slave. Even though Joseph was
a slave,

> the LORD was with Joseph, and he was a successful man;
> and he was in the house of his master the Egyptian. And
> his master saw that the LORD was with him and that the
> LORD made all he did to prosper in his hand. So Joseph
> found favor in his sight, and served him. Then he made
> him overseer of his house, and all that he had he put under
> his authority. So it was, from the time that he had made
> him overseer of his house and all that he had, that the LORD
> blessed the Egyptian's house for Joseph's sake; and the

blessing of the LORD was on all that he had in the house and in the field. Thus he left all that he had in Joseph's hand (Gen. 39:2–6).

Joseph became the overseer of the estate of a prominent Egyptian, which meant that although Joseph did not own it, he had the full run of it. He lived well, ate well, and dressed well. He had all of his material needs met because the Lord caused Potiphar to deal with him favorably.

If you are giving your best effort and are trusting God to give you wisdom in all of your work endeavors, watch for the ways in which the Lord will cause others to bless you.

Note also that the Egyptian was blessed in return. He had no worries or concerns with Joseph managing his household. Joseph had proven himself worthy of his trust. You must give maximum effort and do well in your work, and you must be trustworthy to those who work with you or who supervise you.

The day came, however, when Joseph was falsely accused by Potiphar's wife, and Potiphar had Joseph placed in prison. (Even then, Potiphar was acting with kindness to Joseph; he could have had Joseph killed.) While Joseph was in prison, the Lord again brought him to a place of favor:

But the LORD was with Joseph and showed him mercy, and He gave him favor in the sight of the keeper of the prison. And the keeper of the prison committed to Joseph's hand all the prisoners who were in the prison; whatever they did there, it was his doing. The keeper of the prison did not look into anything that was under Joseph's authority, because the LORD was with him; and whatever he did, the LORD made it prosper (Gen. 39:21–23).

In the end, Joseph was released from prison, and because he had trusted God with his life, had been trustworthy in every circumstance, and had done such good work in the past, the Lord allowed Joseph to be made prime minister of the land, second in command to Pharaoh. Joseph instituted a plan that allowed Egypt to enjoy prosperity in a time of great famine. Even though the famine was severe in Egypt and surrounding countries, Egypt had enough grain in storage that people from other countries came to Egypt for help.

Joseph went from prosperity in one situation to prosperity in another. He never stopped trusting God. He never stopped working. And he never stopped being compensated in ways that were far above what could be expected.

When we place our faith in God and keep His commandments, including His commands to work, we are counted among the righteous. We are in a position to receive God's blessing. David spoke of God's provision to His people:

> *I have been young, and now am old;*
> *Yet I have not seen the righteous forsaken,*
> *Nor his descendants begging bread.*
> *He is ever merciful, and lends;*
> *And his descendants are blessed.*
> *Depart from evil, and do good;*
> *And dwell forevermore.*
> *For the LORD loves justice,*
> *And does not forsake His saints;*
> *They are preserved forever,*
> *But the descendants of the wicked shall be cut off.*
> *The righteous shall inherit the land,*
> *And dwell in it forever (Ps. 37:25–29).*

- *What new insights do you have into work and its rewards?*

- *Can you look back on experiences in your life and see God's compensation plan at work on your behalf?*

- *Specifically, how has your capacity for work increased over the years?*

Our Attitude Toward Work

God desires for you to have several attitudes toward work. Some people seem to believe that their attitude toward work is unimportant as long as they produce well and get a job done. Your attitude toward your work is vital in God's eyes. Your attitude will motivate you to do more than is required, produce at a quality level that is above the expected, and lead you to reap rewards that are greater than you have ever anticipated.

1. Be goal-oriented in your work. Don't approach a job as something you are doing just to pay your bills. See your job as something you have set about to achieve. Set goals for yourself that are beyond the minimum goals required by your employer or others in your field. "Making ends meet" is not a goal. Set a goal that requires you to trust God for abilities, wisdom, insights, and the acquisition of skills that you don't presently have. Set your sights higher than a minimal effort.

The apostle Paul certainly had this attitude when it came to his life and ministry. He wrote to the Philippians,

> Not that I have already attained, or am already perfected; but I press on, that I may lay hold of that for which Christ Jesus has also laid hold of me. Brethren, I do not count myself to have apprehended; but one thing I do, forgetting those things which are behind and reaching forward to those things which are ahead, I press toward the goal for the prize of the upward call of God in Christ Jesus (Phil. 3:12–14).

Paul was "pressing on" even though he was advanced in years and had a long list of accomplishments to his credit. He was still "reaching forward." He was still looking for "the prize of the upward call."

Be as productive as you can be. Do all you know to do. And then trust God to do in you and through you what you cannot do in your own strength.

What the Word Says	What the Word Says to Me
The lazy man will not plow because of winter; He will beg during harvest and have nothing (Prov. 20:4).	_____
Six days you shall labor and do all your work, but the seventh day is the Sabbath of the LORD your God (Ex. 20:9–10).	_____
Whatever your hand finds to do, do it with your might (Eccl. 9:10).	_____

Laziness and slothfulness are two attributes the Lord soundly condemns in His Word. Laziness is a refusal to put forth energy and effort. Being slothful means being wasteful or misusing the resources that are made available to you, including the opportunities that God gives you for work. Both laziness and slothfulness begin with attitude:

- "I don't need to do any more than what I'm doing. Let others do this. I'm going to take my ease."
- "Nobody will know if I take a shortcut or waste this portion. It won't matter if I don't do my best in this instance."

Some of the strongest words in the Bible are against lazy or slothful people. Read this scathing review of the sluggard from Proverbs 6:6–11:

> *Go to the ant, you sluggard!*
> *Consider her ways and be wise,*
> *Which, having no captain,*
> *Overseer or ruler,*
> *Provides her supplies in the summer,*
> *And gathers her food in the harvest.*
> *How long will you slumber, O sluggard?*
> *When will you rise from your sleep?*
> *A little sleep, a little slumber,*
> *A little folding of the hands to sleep—*
> *So shall your poverty come on you like a prowler,*
> *And your need like an armed man.*

Consider also the admonitions against laziness and slothfulness below.

What the Word Says	What the Word Says to Me
The hand of the diligent will rule, But the lazy man will be put to forced labor (Prov. 12:24).	_____ _____ _____
He who is slothful in his work Is a brother to him who is a great destroyer (Prov. 18:9).	_____ _____ _____

2. Have an intense desire to do your best at whatever you undertake. Take pride in your work. Produce the very best quality you can.

The Lord does His work with only one standard: perfection. You, as a finite and limited creation, can never be perfect. Neither can you do perfect work all the time. But you can seek to do better than you have done in the past. You can refuse to settle for a second-class effort or performance.

When you do your best, you have a sense of fulfillment and of joy. You have satisfaction that you have been generous in your effort and in the giving of yourself. And in that, there is reward, both tangible and intangible.

What the Word Says	What the Word Says to Me
Trust in the LORD, and do good (Ps. 37:3).	_____
You shall rejoice in all to which you have put your hand, you and your households, in which the LORD your God has blessed you (Deut. 12:7).	_____

3. *Have a positive attitude toward your work and toward those with whom you work.* It isn't enough that you are productive and do quality work. You also must have an attitude of cooperation with others. Don't judge or condemn your colleagues; don't gossip about them. God will not honor a critical spirit.

Pray for your supervisors, colleagues, vendors, and associates. Look for ways in which you can share the love of Christ with them. At all times you are to be a witness to the work of Christ in your life, and perhaps especially so as you work and in the way you conduct your business affairs.

What the Word Says	What the Word Says to Me
I exhort first of all that supplications, prayers, intercessions, and giving of thanks be made for all men, for kings and all who are in authority, that we may lead a quiet and peaceable life in all godliness and reverence. For this is good and acceptable in the sight of God our Savior, who desires all men to be saved and to come	_____

to the knowledge of the truth (1
Tim. 2:1–4).

[Jesus said,] "Judge not, and you
shall not be judged. Condemn
not, and you shall not be con-
demned. Forgive, and you will be
forgiven" (Luke 6:37).

4. Be determined, persistent, and patient in your work. Believe that you can do the job you have set out to do! Don't expect to succeed or get rich in a day. Don't give up in your good efforts. Don't allow impatience to tempt you to do shoddy work or take shortcuts. Stay true to the course you believe the Lord has set before you, and trust Him to bring you to a safe, satisfying, and rewarding end.

Don't be afraid to try or to take reasonable risks in your work and career. Don't let doubt keep you from pursuing your best. Avoid the temptation to believe, "I don't think God means for me to do any better than I'm doing right now." God always has more for you if you will only believe for more and trust God to enlarge your capacity to do more.

What the Word Says

What the Word Says to Me

Let us not grow weary while doing good, for in due season we
shall reap if we do not lose heart
(Gal. 6:9).

Trust in the LORD with all your
heart,
And lean not on your own under-
standing;
In all your ways acknowledge
Him,

And He shall direct your paths
(Prov. 3:5–6).

_____

_____

I can do all things through
Christ who strengthens me (Phil.
4:13).

_____

_____

_____

Ask God today to guide you in your work:

- To give you the job that's best suited to your talents and abilities, a job through which you can fulfill God's purposes for your life
- To send you the colleagues, clients, associates, employees, customers, and vendors you need
- To give you wisdom in setting policies and establishing procedures related to your work
- To give you strength to do your best, produce the most possible, and achieve all you can
- To help you maintain a high level of quality in all you undertake
- To renew your enthusiasm daily for the jobs and tasks that are set before you
- To honor your efforts from His great storehouse of unlimited supply

I believe God will hear and answer your prayers!

- *What new insights do you have into work and God's plan for your prosperity?*

  _____

  _____

- *In what ways are you feeling challenged today?*

  _____

  _____

LESSON 6

DELIVERANCE FROM DEBT

The Bible leaves no doubt about God's opinion regarding debt. These two are among the foremost verses that deal with this subject, which is a painful one for millions of people:

Owe no one anything except to love one another, for he who loves another has fulfilled the law (Rom. 13:8).

The rich rules over the poor,
And the borrower is servant to the lender (Prov. 22:7).

We are a nation that has ignored these truths. One in five families in our nation is on the brink of bankruptcy. Millions of people are within sixty days of being homeless or in dire financial need. We have bought into a buy-now and pay-later philosophy that has been sold to us for decades by advertisers who tempt us to believe we must have the product they are selling in order to have self-esteem and to project an image of worth. We have swallowed a lie, and we are gagging on it.

God does not want His people to be in debt. The only thing we are to owe others is our love, which we are to give freely and in tangible forms. We are to be givers, not borrowers.

The price for indebtedness can be high indeed. In ancient times, the children of Israel not only lost much of their land and possessions because of debt that accrued, but some sold themselves or their children into slavery in order to pay their debts.

In Nehemiah 5:3–5 we find a mournful outcry from God's people:

> There were also some who said, "We have mortgaged our lands and vineyards and houses, that we might buy grain because of the famine." There were also those who said, "We have borrowed money for the king's tax on our lands and vineyards. Yet now our flesh is as the flesh of our brethren, our children as their children; and indeed we are forcing our sons and our daughters to be slaves, and some of our daughters have been brought into slavery. It is not in our power to redeem them, for other men have our lands and vineyards."

This same heart's cry is voiced by a widow who came to the prophet Elisha and said, "Your servant my husband is dead, and you know that your servant feared the LORD. And the creditor is coming to take my two sons to be his slaves" (2 Kings 4:1).

The husband of this woman, one of the prophets who was associated with Elisha, apparently had died and left his family in debt. The only recourse that seemed available to the woman was to sell her children into slavery to repay what her husband owed.

We may protest, "How horrible! How could a parent sell her children to work off a debt?" And yet that is exactly what we in the United States are doing in strapping our children with a huge national debt. We have gone from being the world's largest creditor nation to debtor status in a matter of only a few decades. What we have done on a national scale we have also done on an individual and family scale. Our children will be forced to pay for our foolishness.

God is so opposed to debt that He doesn't even want His people to be the security for another person's debt—in our language today, that might mean being the cosigner on a loan:

> *Do not be one of those who shakes hands in a pledge [signifying a loan],*
> *One of those who is surety for debts;*
> *If you have nothing with which to pay,*
> *Why should he take away your bed from under you? (Prov. 22:26–27).*

In other words, God doesn't want you to be faced with the possibility of paying another person's debt, a situation that could put your livelihood and possessions into jeopardy—in this case, even your bed!

- *In your life, have you been in debt, or are you now in debt?*

  _____

  _____

- *How does debt make you feel?*

  _____

  _____

- *When you are free of debt, how do you feel?*

  _____

  _____

- *How do you feel about God's admonition that you should be free of debt?*

  _____

  _____

The Relationship of Debt to Faith

Why is God so opposed to debt for His people?

There are a number of reasons. Debt has a negative impact upon the spiritual life. Some of the reasons God is opposed to debt can be discovered when we take a look at the reasons people get into debt:

People get into debt because they buy things they can't afford. Credit cards are bad for many people. They are overused, misused, and abused. Buying with a credit card is taking out a loan, however short-term it may be. Unless you can manage credit cards wisely, I suggest that you wean yourself away from them completely.

When we buy things we can't afford, we are saying to God, "I need this more than I need to be free of debt." We make many credit card purchases so we can bolster self-esteem. We trust in things to give us a sense of identity and well-being rather than trust God for our identity.

Furthermore, when we buy on credit, we aren't trusting God to give us the things we need *in His timing*. We want what we want *now*. God's plan often requires us to wait for certain things, not only so that we are able to receive them, use them fully, and use them wisely, but also so that others can benefit from God's gifts to us. Trust God for His timing in the blessings you receive. James 1:4 states, "Let patience have its perfect work, that you may be perfect and complete, lacking nothing."

People are in debt because they make unwise investments. God promises to give His people insight, answers, and direction. All we need to do is ask Him for these things, and wait until we are assured of His response. James 1:5–6 advises us, "If any of you lacks wisdom, let him ask of God, who gives to all liberally and without reproach, and it will be given to him. But let him ask in faith, with no doubting."

Too few people turn to God to ask His advice about the investments and major purchases they make, such as homes, cars, and other big-ticket items. Others fail to seek God's advice before they enter into partnerships or business opportunities that require them to sign contracts or make financial commitments. I firmly believe that when we ask God for His wisdom, He will give us clear leading about what to avoid and what to pursue. He can see the ending from the beginning, and He knows what will be best for us now and in the future.

People are in debt because they are careless in their purchases, making unwise or unnecessary choices. Much of what we buy we don't need and, in many cases, don't really want six months or a year later. Fashions change. Fads come and go. And although I am not advocating that we be old-fashioned or outdated in our dress or possessions, we should always seek to buy quality items that will last. Again, we need to seek God's wisdom.

People are in debt because they lack forethought for the future. I have met Christian people who believe they are to live in the moment and never have a savings account, much less provide an inheritance for their children. I disagree.

The Bible has very positive things to say about inheritance. For example, when Isaac called Jacob and blessed him, he said to him,

> *May God Almighty bless you,*
> *And make you fruitful and multiply you . . .*
> *That you may inherit the land*
> *In which you are a stranger,*
> *Which God gave to Abraham (Gen. 28:3–4).*

Isaac had inherited the land from his father, Abraham, and in turn, was handing it down to his son. If either Abraham or Isaac had lived only for himself and for the moment, and in the process had squandered what he had, he would have had no inheritance to pass on.

Proverbs 13:22 declares, "A good man leaves an inheritance to his children's children." Again, a person who lacks forethought for the future leaves no inheritance.

In the parable of Jesus about the prodigal son and the loving father, we read about a son who squandered his inheritance, becoming so deeply in debt that his only recourse was to hire himself out to work in the hog pens of a faraway country. He was a young man who had no forethought for the future. (See Luke 15:11–32.)

People are in debt because they lose a job or miss work owing to illness or injury. There may be little that you can do to immunize yourself against a job loss, injury, or illness, but if you have saved a portion of your earnings, you are likely to have a financial cushion to see you through hard times. Debt only compounds the pain and emotional trauma that you and your entire family experience when a member of your family is unable to work to help provide for the family's needs. It is easy during times of job loss or serious accident or illness to fall into depression, doubt, or discouragement. You will be less likely to experience these faith-debilitating emotions if you have financial means to pay your bills until you are able to work again.

It is far easier to stay out of debt than to get out of debt. Make a decision that you are going to follow God's plan in your finances and that you are not going to fall prey to the alluring messages that tempt you to borrow, buy beyond your means, or spend your money unwisely.

• *In your experience, how has debt affected your faith?*

_____

_____

How Much Debt Is Too Much?

How far in debt is too deep?

Much of our society is based upon thirty-, forty-five-, or sixty-day pay cycles. I don't believe that owing a bill for a few days or weeks is tantamount to debt.

Debt is financial bondage. You know that you are in debt when you

- can't pay bills as they come due.
- start putting off the payment of one bill in order to pay another.
- feel pressure regarding your bills.
- become worried about how you will pay your bills.
- start looking for quick fixes or quick ways out of your debt.

If you don't feel at ease and confident when you look at your financial situation, you are in debt.

Debt can lead to a host of attitudes that affect your spiritual life negatively.

First, debt creates an internal pressure that may be described as stress, anxiety, worry, or deep frustration. The person who suffers from these emotions does not have a heart fully turned toward God. Debt can also become a mental preoccupation—your first and last thoughts each day are about whom you owe, how much you owe, and what you can do about what you owe. You are not in a position to hear from God about His priorities for the use of your time and resources.

Ultimately, unpaid debt can lead to fear—a deep anxiety that you will never be out of debt. Fear is the opposite of faith.

Second, debt places a strain on family relationships. Money concerns are among the primary causes of family arguments. Mismanagement of money can smother love.

Don't allow that to happen in your home! When disagreements upset or interrupt the free flow of loving communication in your home, you are facing a problem that has spiritual dimensions to it.

Third, debt causes you to become resentful of others. Rather than reach out to others, you begin to avoid those you owe and, at times, those you think know about your indebtedness. Debt can cause you to distrust or look unkindly upon those who seem to have no money problems. It can cause you to become envious. These are not godly attitudes.

Fourth, debt hurts the testimony of a Christian. It is difficult to declare to the world that you are trusting God to meet all of your needs and to be deeply in debt at the same time. Your credibility is destroyed.

- *In your experience, what attitudes did you find yourself developing as a consequence of your debt?*

_____

_____

Debt affects your spiritual life in a negative way because debt keeps you from listening totally to God's directives for your daily life. You lose much of your flexibility when you allow yourself to become burdened by debt.

When you are in debt, you must be concerned about the payment of that debt. That concern rightfully becomes a major priority in your life. In the process, you are no longer free to act immediately should God direct you to do so.

- *Has a debt ever kept you from being flexible in responding to God's call on your life?*

_____

_____

The Obligation to Pay Debts

You may be tempted if you are in debt to walk away from your indebtedness, justifying your action so that you might be free to follow God's call or to place more emphasis on your spiritual life. Walking away from a debt is not scriptural. Psalm 37:21 states very clearly:

> *The wicked borrows and does not repay,*
> *But the righteous shows mercy and gives.*

We have an obligation to pay our debts. And God will help us pay them if we will turn to Him and trust Him for the wisdom about how to pay our debts.

Two effective examples appear in God's Word. Both involve the prophet Elisha. In the first example, the sons of the prophets desired to have a larger place to live so they asked permission of Elisha to go to the river and cut some beams to make a new home for themselves. Elisha granted them permission and also agreed with their request to go along with them to the river.

As one of the men was cutting down a tree, "the iron ax head fell into the water; and he cried out and said, 'Alas, master! For it was borrowed.'" (See 2 Kings 6:1–5.) Iron was a rare commodity to the children of Israel. The Philistines had control over the natural resources needed for the making of iron tools and chariots. An iron ax head was costly and not easily replaced. The man recognized without hesitation that—accident or not—he had an obligation to restore the ax head. It was an obligation he could not meet.

God revealed to Elisha what he should do to regain the ax head. A miracle was involved, the ax head was recovered, and the indebtedness was resolved.

I believe it is important in this incident to note that the man was not foolish in his actions. He was working honestly and in good faith when the accident happened that caused the ax head to be lost. I believe God comes to the aid of those who experience debt in this way. Conversely, I do not believe God gives us any promise of a miracle to absolve us of debt that is accrued because of our sin, willful disobedience, or foolishness. He will help us get out of debt in these instances, but He does not miraculously restore our loss or lack.

The second miracle related to indebtedness and Elisha is one we have already touched upon. The widow who came to Elisha in concern that her sons were about to be sold to her husband's creditors received godly advice from Elisha about what she should do. Elisha told her to borrow (only temporarily) all the vessels she could from her friends and neighbors, and then to shut herself away in her home with her two sons. Together they were to begin to pour oil from the only jar of oil they had remaining in their possession. God sovereignly and miraculously multiplied the oil to fill all the vessels they had gathered. The money gained from the sale of that oil was sufficient to pay the debt and to give the family the necessary money to live. (See 2 Kings 4:1–7.)

In one case, God immediately recovered a potential loss. In the other case, God required the woman and her sons to take specific steps (which involved work and management of existing resources). I don't know how God will deal with you in resolving your indebtedness, but I believe this: He has a plan for helping you get out of debt. It may take a miracle, but God is a miracle worker. Seek His counsel.

Also in the examples we've noted, both the prophet's son and the prophet's widow had the good sense to seek out godly counsel as they faced their financial difficulty. We are wise to do the same.

I encourage you to read these two passages of Scripture in their entirety and to note other insights you have into how these people were helped in paying their debt.

What the Word Says	What the Word Says to Me
The widow's miracle supply of oil (2 Kings 4:1–7).	_____ _____
The ax head that floated (2 Kings 6:1–7).	_____ _____

One of the ways in which God helps us to be free of debt is to give us an opportunity to increase our income. That opportunity may come in the form of a new job or a part-time job to augment the one we currently have.

Some people jump quickly to the conclusion that the primary solution for their debt is to earn more money. That isn't always the case. The truth is, unless you change your habits and attitudes that got you into debt in the first place, an increase in income isn't likely to resolve your problem. You are likely to be in even greater debt, thinking that you now have the ability to pay your old bills and take on new ones.

Again, ask the Lord to give you His wisdom in the matter of your income.

- *What new insights do you have into debt and its relationship to your spiritual life?*

_____
_____

As You Face Your Debts

As you face your debts today, whether large or small . . .
Be resolved within yourself that you will pay your debts. Don't

seek to escape them. Don't ignore them. Set a goal date for the payment of each bill. Work steadily, consistently, and patiently toward full payment of what you owe.

Thank God for His help as you pay off each bill. Make the payment of your debts an opportunity for praise. Don't complain about the bills that remain or criticize yourself or others for your indebtedness.

Review your financial expenditures weekly. Take a long look at how you became a victim of debt, and make the necessary changes in your credit card, borrowing, and spending habits.

Once you are free from debt . . .

Praise God for helping you to be free of the financial bondage you have experienced. Ask for God's continual help so that you might live debt-free for the rest of your life. Trust Him to guide you and to help you.

- *In what ways are you being challenged by God today?*

  _____

  _____

LESSON 7

THE KEY TO UNLOCKING PROSPERITY

PART 1

A lack of work (laziness), debt, and bad attitudes or bad habits related to money are major reasons that people do not enjoy the prosperity God desires for them. The number one reason, however, in my opinion, is that people withhold from God.

They withhold their hearts and their wills, refusing to obey God's principles. They stubbornly seek to make their own decisions, refusing to avail themselves of God's wisdom. They withhold what they do have in the way of resources, refusing to let loose of any of it because they don't trust God to provide for them.

Stingy, self-centered, closed-off-from-God people cannot prosper. It is like asking a turtle to walk to freedom and security while it is all closed up inside its shell. It can't be done.

Being open to God involves both giving to and receiving from God. We give Him our lives, our praise, our thanksgiving, our abilities, our resources, and we ask God to use us. God uses us when we make ourselves available to Him, and He blesses us in returning to us all that we need physically, emotionally, psychologically, mentally, and materially. When we are open in our giving of ourselves to God, we are generally open to receiving from God.

The person who closes himself off from God may want things from God, but he wants them only in a getting mode. Usually, that person wants only very specific things from God. This is not true receiving.

When we receive from God, we are open to receiving all that He has for us, and whatever He has for us, with a thankful heart. There is no true receiving from God without the balance of giving to God. It's like having a wide-open door that allows passage in both directions.

God doesn't want merely your money. Many people think that. They see God as having a giant hand extended toward them, ready to take whatever they have. That picture cannot be supported with Scripture. It is the notion of selfish humankind.

God wants all of you. He wants a life totally and completely committed to Him in love and service, a life dedicated to doing things God's way and to being God's person on this earth. God wants a relationship with you that holds nothing back. And in return, He desires to hold nothing of Himself back from you.

Who gets the better end of this covenant relationship? You do, of course. You are a finite, imperfect person. God receives you as you are. He gives you in return all of who He is—infinite, perfect. He asks you to receive Him in fullness. And when you do, friend, you can't help prospering.

- *In your experience, can you point to times in which you have been open fully to God? What were the results? How did you feel?*

  _____

  _____

- *Have there been times when you have been closed to God? What were the results? How did you feel?*

_____

_____

Three Reasons You Withhold from God

There are three main reasons you withhold your life, including your resources, from God. All of them have deeply spiritual ramifications.

1. You want to do things your own way. You act out of human pride. You want what you want, and you want to keep everything you believe you have earned. Rebellion against God's plan and principles is always an expression of personal pride. The basis for pride is that you think you are somebody, and that you have acquired the substance of your life, apart from God. Nothing could be farther from the truth.

Everything that you have comes from God—all of your talents, your good ideas, your energy, your very life's breath. You may think you exist and act and produce and acquire apart from God, but you don't.

God cannot bless a proud heart. Such a heart is closed to God's work. The rebellious person is in no position to become prosperous.

What the Word Says	What the Word Says to Me
A father of the fatherless, a defender of widows, Is God in His holy habitation. God sets the solitary in families; He brings out those who are bound into prosperity; But the rebellious dwell in a dry land (Ps. 68:5–6).	_____ _____ _____ _____ _____ _____ _____
"Woe to the rebellious children,"	_____

says the LORD,
"Who take counsel, but not of
Me,
And who devise plans, but not of
My Spirit,
That they may add sin to sin;
Who walk to go down to Egypt,
And have not asked My advice,
To strengthen themselves in the
strength of Pharaoh,
And to trust in the shadow of
Egypt!
Therefore the strength of Pha-
raoh
Shall be your shame,
And trust in the shadow of Egypt
Shall be your humiliation" (Isa.
30:1–3).

"Like keepers of a field they are
against her all around,
Because she has been rebellious
against Me," says the LORD.
"Your ways and your doings
Have procured these things for
you.
This is your wickedness,
Because it is bitter,
Because it reaches to your heart"
(Jer. 4:17–18).

Pride goes before destruction,
And a haughty spirit before a fall
(Prov. 16:18).

A man's pride will bring him low,   _____
But the humble in spirit will re-   _____
tain honor (Prov. 29:23).   _____

2. You have unbelief. A second reason you withhold your life and substance from God is that you don't trust God to provide for you or to take care of you. You refuse to believe that God's promises and principles apply to you personally. You think you have to do it yourself because God either can't or won't.

Again, nothing could be farther from the truth. You will come quickly to the end of yourself—to the end of your ability, the end of your manufactured happiness, the end of your energy and physical resources, the end of your power, the end of your knowledge, the end of your life. When you trust in yourself, you trust in someone who is frail, weak, and temporary—no matter how strong and great you may think of yourself at the moment.

When you trust in God, however, you put your trust in Someone who is all-powerful, all-knowing, and eternal. He doesn't fail. He doesn't change. In God is the greatest security you can ever know.

Jesus gave you a beautiful image to hold in your mind anytime you are tempted to think that you cannot trust God to take care of you:

> Consider the ravens, for they neither sow nor reap, which have neither storehouse nor barn; and God feeds them. Of how much more value are you than the birds? And which of you by worrying can add one cubit to his stature? If you then are not able to do the least, why are you anxious for the rest? Consider the lilies, how they grow: they neither toil nor spin; and yet I say to you, even Solomon in all his glory was not arrayed like one of these. If then God so clothes the grass, which today is in the field and tomorrow is thrown into the oven, how much more will He clothe you, O you of little faith? And do not seek what you should eat or what you should drink, nor have an anxious mind. For all these things the nations of the world seek after, and your Father knows that you need these things. But seek the

kingdom of God, and all these things shall be added to you. Do not fear, little flock, for it is your Father's good pleasure to give you the kingdom (Luke 12:24–32).

As you read through the verses below, relate them to your personal prosperity in the Lord.

What the Word Says	What the Word Says to Me
For the LORD God is a sun and shield;	_____
The LORD will give grace and glory;	_____
No good thing will He withhold From those who walk uprightly.	_____
O LORD of hosts, Blessed is the man who trusts in You! (Ps. 84:11–12).	_____
O Israel, trust in the LORD; He is their help and their shield.	_____
O house of Aaron, trust in the LORD;	_____
He is their help and their shield.	_____
You who fear the LORD, trust in the LORD;	_____
He is their help and their shield.	_____
The LORD has been mindful of us;	_____
He will bless us; He will bless the house of Israel; He will bless the house of Aaron.	_____
He will bless those who fear the LORD, Both small and great.	_____

May the LORD give you increase
more and more,
You and your children.
May you be blessed by the LORD,
Who made heaven and earth (Ps.
115:9–15).

He who trusts in his riches will
fall,
But the righteous will flourish
like foliage (Prov. 11:28).

_____
_____
_____
_____
_____
_____

_____
_____
_____
_____

3. You are unthankful. You may withhold yourself from God
because you have an ungrateful heart. You know deep inside that
God is sovereign and the Source of your life. You believe in God
and trust Him to the best of your ability. But then you never give
Him a word of thanks. You never open your mouth to praise Him
or to acknowledge His work in your life.

How is this withholding from God? When you fail to voice your
thanksgiving and praise to God, you fail to give to God what God
is rightfully due. God is worthy of praise. He alone is worthy of
praise! In fact, Jesus noted that if you don't praise the Lord, the
very stones will cry out to do so. (See Luke 19:40.)

God desires your praise not because it satisfies any need in Him,
but because it opens you up to receive from God. When you praise
God, you have a much clearer understanding of who He is, and
who you are, and a much greater appreciation of all that He has
done for you. Praise keeps you cleansed of pride. It keeps you in a
right relationship with God.

What the Word Says

As He was now drawing near the
descent of the Mount of Olives,
the whole multitude of the disciples

What the Word Says to Me

_____
_____
_____
_____

began to rejoice and praise God
with a loud voice for all the
mighty works they had seen, saying:
"Blessed is the King who comes
in the name of the LORD!
Peace in heaven and glory in the
highest!"
And some of the Pharisees called
to Him from the crowd,
"Teacher, rebuke Your disciples." But He answered and said
to them, "I tell you that if these
should keep silent, the stones
would immediately cry out"
(Luke 19:37–40).

I will love You, O LORD, my
strength,
The LORD is my rock and my for-
tress and my deliverer;
My God, my strength, in whom I
will trust;
My shield and the horn of my salvation, my stronghold.
I will call upon the LORD, who is
worthy to be praised;
So shall I be saved from my enemies (Ps. 18:1–3).

You are worthy, O Lord,
To receive glory and honor and
power;
For You created all things,

And by Your will they exist and
were created (Rev. 4:11).   _____
                                             _____

Surely the righteous shall give   _____
thanks to Your name;   _____
The upright shall dwell in Your   _____
presence (Ps. 140:13).   _____

The Lord simply does not prosper anyone who is rebellious, proud, unbelieving, or unthankful. Such a person has closed herself to God and, therefore, is in no position to receive from God.

Ask the Lord today to keep you from pride.

Ask the Lord today to help you trust Him more.

Praise the Lord today for all that He has done for you, in you, and through you, and praise Him for His many promises of good things yet to come.

Withholding Our Substance from God

A part of withholding yourself from the Lord invariably includes withholding your substance from God. You miss out on prosperity when you do not give of your material goods—your money, your financial resources, your gain, your substance—to God.

It is not enough that you give God your heart, time, energy, talents, and strength. Your material substance is a part of you. In many ways, it is a *tangible* expression of *intangible* time, energy, talents, and ability. You have what you hold in your hands because God has given you the ability to earn it; money is earned in exchange for time and skills. Money is a part of you, both in the earning of it and in the giving of it. You must be as generous in your material gifts as you are in every other area.

Giving to God opens up the financial area of your life to God. If you want to be blessed financially, you must be generous in your finances. As is true in every other area of life, the degree to which you open up yourself to God in giving is the degree to which you open up yourself to God for receiving. If you are closed to God in your finances, you are also closed to God in reaping financial blessing.

Remind yourself of the verses below, some of which also appear in other lessons. They relate not only to finances but also to every area of life.

What the Word Says	What the Word Says to Me
Do not be deceived, God is not mocked; for whatever a man sows, that he will also reap (Gal. 6:7).	_____ _____ _____ _____
He who sows sparingly will also reap sparingly, and he who sows bountifully will also reap bountifully (2 Cor. 9:6).	_____ _____ _____ _____ _____
[Jesus said,] "Give, and it will be given to you. . . . with the same measure that you use, it will be measured back to you" (Luke 6:38).	_____ _____ _____ _____ _____
[Jesus said,] "Freely you have received, freely give" (Matt. 10:8).	_____ _____

- *What new insights do you have into the way to prosperity?*

_____

_____

- *In what ways is the Lord challenging you today?*

_____

_____

LESSON 8

THE KEY TO UNLOCKING PROSPERITY

PART 2

God has set forth very specific directives about what He expects us to give to Him of our financial substance. One of the clearest Bible passages about this is Malachi 3:8–12:

> *"Will a man rob God?*
> *Yet you have robbed Me!*
> *But you say,*
> *'In what way have we robbed You?'*
> *In tithes and offerings.*
> *You are cursed with a curse,*
> *For you have robbed Me,*
> *Even this whole nation.*
> *Bring all the tithes into the storehouse,*
> *That there may be food in My house,*
> *And try Me now in this,"*
> *Says the LORD of hosts,*

> *"If I will not open for you the windows of heaven*
> *And pour out for you such blessing*
> *That there will not be room enough to receive it.*
> *And I will rebuke the devourer for your sakes,*
> *So that he will not destroy the fruit of your ground,*
> *Nor shall the vine fail to bear fruit for you in the field,"*
> *Says the LORD of hosts;*
> *"And all nations will call you blessed,*
> *For you will be a delightful land,"*
> *Says the LORD of hosts.*

A Passage in Malachi

Let's take a close look at several key concepts presented in this passage.

Tithes and Offerings

This passage gives us God's directive as to how much He expects we will give to Him—the tithe, which is 10 percent. (The word *tithe* is based on the number ten in Hebrew; ten is also the number in Hebrew associated with the concept of increase or multiplied blessing.)

Offerings were gifts, often of material goods, that were given above and beyond the tithe. Offerings were usually made for specific reasons—to meet a special need in the nation or in thanksgiving for a special blessing. For example, the children of Israel gave an offering at the time the tabernacle was constructed. They gave so generously that Moses actually had to tell them to stop giving! (See Ex. 35:4–36:7.)

The tithe was expected to be the first tenth of what a person had received. If we were counting out pennies, we would say, "One for God, nine for me. One for God, nine for me." At no time in the Scriptures is the first tenth considered to belong rightfully to anyone other than God.

The tithe is given to God *from* our increase and *for* our increase. It is the way we open the door of our finances to give and then to receive God's blessing.

We should always keep in mind that God gives us this tenth in the first place. It never is ours. Remember the words of 1 Chronicles 29:14: "All things come from You, and of Your own we have given You." When we give the first tenth of our earnings back to God, we return to Him what was His in the first place, and what He asks us to give to Him so that He might give us even more. The tithe is our way to renew God's blessing into our lives. It is always for our increase.

This cyclical aspect of giving is well stated in Isaiah 55:10–11:

> *For as the rain comes down,*
> *and the snow from heaven,*
> *And do not return there,*
> *But water the earth,*
> *And make it bring forth and bud,*
> *That it may give seed to the sower*
> *And bread to the eater,*
> *So shall My word be that goes forth from My mouth;*
> *It shall not return to Me void,*
> *But it shall accomplish what I please,*
> *And it shall prosper in the thing for which I sent it.*

God gives you His blessings—including material provision—and whatever He gives to you has embedded within it the seed that triggers even more blessing. Just as the rain and snow cause the plants to grow and produce for your benefit, just as His Word has the potential to produce faith in your heart, so His material blessing has the potential to bring you even greater blessing. If you hoard that seed of potential blessing and keep it for yourself, it will not produce. You cannot make that seed, or any other seed, grow. Only God can cause a seed of any kind to multiply on your behalf.

Read what God says about the tithe elsewhere in His Word.

What the Word Says	What the Word Says to Me
All the tithe of the land, whether of the seed of the land or of the	_____ _____

fruit of the tree, is the LORD's. It
is holy to the LORD.
... And concerning the tithe of
the herd or the flock, of whatever
passes under the rod, the tenth
one shall be holy to the LORD
(Lev. 27:30, 32).

You shall seek the place where
the LORD your God chooses, out
of all your tribes, to put His name
for His dwelling place; and there
you shall go. There you shall take
your burnt offerings, your sacri-
fices, your tithes, the heave offerings of your hand, your vowed
offerings, your freewill offerings,
and the firstborn of your herds
and flocks. And there you shall
eat before the LORD your God,
and you shall rejoice in all to
which you have put your hand,
you and your households, in
which the LORD your God has
blessed you (Deut. 12:5–7).

Honor the LORD with your possessions,
And with the firstfruits of all
your increase;
So your barns will be filled with
plenty,
And your vats will overflow with
new wine (Prov. 3:9–10).

The giving of tithes and offerings was to be marked by joy; the presenting of tithes and offerings was a celebration in response to what God had given and in anticipation of what God would give.

- *How do you feel when you hear the word* tithe?

_____

_____

The Lord is very specific in the way we are to give our tithes and offerings.

First, we are to bring our tithes and offerings into His storehouse— generally that meant His tabernacle or His temple in the Old Testament, and the church in the New Testament. Our tithes are to be given to the place in our lives where we participate in the worship of the Lord. It is to be a place with His name on it, not a mere charitable work, but a work that bears the Lord's name.

Second, we are to make our gifts on a regular basis. Paul advised the Corinthians (as well as all the churches of Galatia), "On the first day of the week let each one of you lay something aside, storing up as he may prosper, that there be no collections when I come" (1 Cor. 16:2). The giving of the believers was to be a regular part of their weekly worship service.

Third, we are to make our gifts joyfully. People who give grudgingly, solely from a sense of obligation and duty, are not truly opening up their entire lives to God's prosperity. Hear the words of Paul to the Corinthians:

> So let each one give as he purposes in his heart, not grudgingly or of necessity; for God loves a cheerful giver. And God is able to make all grace abound toward you, that you, always having all sufficiency in all things, may have an abundance for every good work (2 Cor. 9:7–8).

The joy in our hearts about giving is a direct expression of our trust in God to meet our needs.

"But," you may ask, "all of these references to tithing are in the

Old Testament. I'm a New Testament believer, and I don't see much about tithing in the New Testament."

There is a reason for that. Jesus certainly taught that we are to give

- to the needy (Matt. 25:37–40).
- sacrificially (Mark 12:41–44).
- without a great public display or show (Matt. 6:1–4).
- and expect to receive in proportion to what we give (Luke 6:38).
- knowing that it is more blessed to give than to receive (Acts 20:35).

Why didn't Jesus teach about tithing? Because the people were already tithing. Tithing was deeply ingrained in the fabric of the society in which Jesus ministered. There was no reason to preach about something the people were already doing. In fact, the deeply religious Pharisees were tithing the herbs that grew in their gardens. Jesus didn't decry their tithing in that manner; instead He approved of their tithing and said they were to place greater importance on bigger issues: God's justice and the love of God. He said, "You tithe mint and rue and all manner of herbs, and pass by justice and the love of God. These you ought to have done, without leaving the others undone" (Luke 11:42).

The first-century Christians were giving Christians. They tithed to the storehouse of the Lord, and in some cases, they sacrificed all that they had for the benefit of their brothers and sisters in Christ. (See Acts 4:34–37.) The early Christians did not balk at the requirement to give. They rejoiced in the opportunity.

- *What new insights do you have into tithing?*

_____

_____

Romans 12:8 speaks of a ministry of giving that flows from a divine gift of giving. Paul tells those who have this ministry or gift of giving to give "with liberality."

Those who are called to such a ministry go beyond the giving of tithes and offerings. They are often blessed in unusual and abundant ways so they can give great sums to the work of the Lord. Sometimes they are blessed for a season in their lives so they can give special gifts to particular works or ministries. I know of a man who reached a point in his life where he was giving God 90 percent of what he earned and living off the remaining 10 percent. His income had grown so vast over the years of faithful giving that he was able to live a very fine life on the 10 percent. He channeled everything else into the work of the Lord. This man, in my opinion, had a gift of giving.

Robbing God

Few of us would ever think of robbing God. We tend to regard the withholding of our money from God as resulting in benefit to ourselves—that we haven't lost access to a portion of our earnings or money. We rarely see our failure to give as robbing God. Yet God says that when we withhold our tithes and offerings, we are robbing Him. How can this be?

The tithe belongs to God. It is holy. (See Lev. 27:30.) It is sanctified—set apart—and rightfully belongs to God. When we take God's portion of our earnings and use it for ourselves, we are taking what does not belong to us. God cannot bless thieves.

When you really stop to think about it, it is foolish to try to steal from God. God knows that you have what you have, He knows where to find you and your resources, and He knows when and where you attempt to hide from God what is His. In attempting to cheat God, you are cheating yourself. You are cutting yourself off from the abundance He desires to give you.

Food in God's House

In Malachi, we read that we are to bring our tithes into God's storehouse so that there might be food in God's house—in other words, so that there might be sustenance and nourishment useful for life and growth.

Can you imagine what would happen in our churches and in our nation if every Christian tithed on a regular basis? There would be an enormous amount of money for spreading the gospel and helping needy people. Outreach programs to poor, homeless, sick, and destitute people would be fully funded. Christian charities would have the money they need and would not have to spend their time or resources on fund-raising. Missionaries and evangelistic missions would be fully supported. The increased proclamation of the gospel would have a tremendous impact on strengthening the moral fiber of our nation, and especially on strengthening our families. The net result would be far less need and far less crime in our society, which could translate into lower taxes, less dependence on programs such as Social Security and Medicare, and less expensive bureaucracy.

The tithe doesn't evaporate into thin air. It is used to benefit people in need and to support those who minister directly to the needy people. It is used for programs that give life and hope to those in need. The tithe comes back to us indirectly by giving us healthier and more vibrant communities (both churches and neighborhoods) in which to live and do our work.

Malachi said that the nation of Israel was under a curse because it had robbed God of tithes and offerings. Are we any different today?

A Test of God's Faithfulness

God almost dares us in this passage of Malachi to put His faithfulness to the test. He says, "Try Me now in this." In other words, "Put Me to the test. Check it out for yourself."

God has given us a system that is so easy even a child can do it. Are we willing to give God 10 percent on a regular basis and see what happens?

A Blessing from Heaven

God promises to the one who brings tithes and offerings into His storehouse that He will open the windows of heaven and "pour out for you such blessing/That there will not be room enough to receive it." What form will that blessing take? I believe it is different for each person. God's blessing certainly comes to us in the form of

- an abundance of strength, energy, and physical vitality and health.
- an abundance of innovative, creative ideas and insights.
- a renewed joy and positive attitude.
- an enhanced ability to communicate with others and work with them.
- provision from unexpected sources.
- new opportunities for work and investment.

- *In your experience, in what forms have you received blessings from the open windows of heaven?*

_____

_____

Furthermore, God says that the blessing He will pour out of heaven is so great that you will not be able to contain it. Have you ever enjoyed a blessing that great? That's a spill-over, abundant, more-than-enough, extravagant, beyond-mere-need blessing. And again, note what happens: this increase overflows from your life to bless others. When you prosper, everybody around you is brought to a higher level of prosperity, including those who have a lack in their lives.

A Rebuke to the Devourer

Not only does God promise an overflowing blessing, but He says He will "rebuke the devourer." Your work will come to fruition. You will be spared from attacks of the enemy against your life.

In very practical ways, a rebuke to the devourer can mean

- less illness—less susceptibility to viruses and disease-causing bacteria.
- fewer breakdowns in equipment, machinery, or vehicles.
- fewer obstacles or problems encountered.
- fewer interruptions, delays, or detours.
- fewer accidents or mishaps.

All of that can result in fewer lost days at work, less stress, and lower expenses.

Not only do you experience a beneficial increase when you give your tithes and offerings, but you experience a decrease in things that cause you loss, injury, or harm. The net effect is an altogether positive one!

There is another way to look at this: the 90 percent that is remaining after you give God His 10 percent will have the blessing of God on it. It will be a full 90 percent that has the potential to bring great reward. Believe me, I would rather have 90 percent with God's blessing on it than 100 percent without God's blessing.

- *In your life, how have you experienced a "rebuke of the devourer" for your sake?*

_____

_____

Honor

When you bring all your tithes and offerings into God's storehouse, you experience the reward of a good reputation. The Lord says, "And all nations will call you blessed." In other words, your life will be enviable. Others will speak well of you and want to be like you.

This directly relates to your Christian witness. When people see you prospering, they will gravitate toward you. They will want to know your secret. They will want to have the joy you have, the feeling of fulfillment and meaning you enjoy, the blessings that you are experiencing. You will find it easier than ever in your life to share the gospel of Jesus Christ with others.

- *In your experience, have you found it easier to witness for Christ when you are prosperous or in need?*

_____

_____

Four Promises

The giving of tithes and offerings holds out these four promises in Malachi:

1. The promise of prosperity—the windows of heaven will be opened to you.

2. The promise of plenty—you will have a blessing that is not only sufficient, but overflowing.

3. The promise of protection—the devourer will be rebuked for your sake.

4. The promise of personal testimony—you will have an expanded witness for the Lord.

- *How do you feel about these promises?*

   _____

   _____

- *In what ways are you feeling challenged?*

   _____

   _____

Given these promises of God toward the giving of your tithes and offerings, and given the alternatives if you don't give, you should be eager to give to God what is rightfully His! You should be excited and enthusiastic about giving—not merely so that you might receive financial blessing but so that you can receive God's presence.

With God's blessing, you always receive God's presence. Your relationship with Him grows richer, deeper, more meaningful, and more intimate. God's blessings are bestowed upon you so that God might prove Himself faithful to you and so that He might draw you ever nearer to Himself. That is the greatest reward you can ever know.

A Life That Is Above and Beyond

I have never tithed. Let me hasten to explain. In my first job, I made $4 a week as a newspaper boy. I brought $1 a week to God's storehouse. I never would have dreamed of limiting myself to a mere $0.40. I was so grateful for the job and so pleased to be earning $4, it never crossed my mind to give less than $1. Shortly thereafter, I got a job—also as a newspaper boy—for $20 a week. Talk about the windows of heaven opening to me! That was a fivefold increase in my income! I gave back far more than 10 percent a week to the church.

While I had that job, a man offered to help me get into and attend college. I went to college with $75 in my pocket, and I left college not owing a cent. God richly and abundantly met my need. Once I had only a dime in my pocket, but I was never completely without money. And I never gave *only* 10 percent of what I received to God. I was in relationship with a God of abundance. I never would have dreamed of giving back to Him only a bare minimum.

My giving was born of gratitude and thanksgiving that He should do so much for me. My only regrets were that I couldn't give more to the work of the Lord.

I know from personal experience that God is a God of blessing. He doesn't want your money as some kind of payback for blessing you. He wants *you*. He wants you to want Him. He wants you to open up your life so that your entire existence is one of generous giving and abundant receiving. He wants you to grow, develop, and prosper in every area of your life. Our God is a loving God who desires your utmost and highest.

Are you willing to trust Him today with your money and material resources? The key to unlocking prosperity—including financial prosperity—lies in what you give.

- *What new insights do you have into the giving of tithes and offerings?*

- *In what ways are you being challenged by God today to unlock greater prosperity in your life?*

LESSON 9

DANGER SIGNALS

Y ou can lose the blessings that God gives you. Prosperity is not necessarily a lasting or constant state of being. It is not enough to know how to become prosperous in God's eyes, you must also learn how to *stay* prosperous. It is only as you live in prosperity that you truly can become an outstanding steward of all that God gives you. Keeping prosperity is certainly at the heart of good financial stewardship.

God gives only good gifts. Another way of saying this might be: all God's gifts are good. But equally true is the fact that we can misuse all of God's good gifts. Food is a necessity. But too much food can make us fat, which in turn can contribute to disease. Likewise medicines are good, but taken in excess or in wrong combination, they can cause harm. Affection is wonderful, but directed inappropriately, it can destroy a family.

We must be very cautious to use the blessings that God has given us for good and not evil.

- *Can you think of an example in your life or in the life of a person you know in which a blessing of God became harmful through misuse or abuse? What were the consequences?*

_____

_____

Five Attitudes That Eat Away at Prosperity

Five attitudes can destroy prosperity, usually bit by bit until all of a blessing we have received has been put in jeopardy or has been eaten away.

1. Covetousness

Covetousness can also be defined as greed. In an earlier lesson we discussed how greed can keep us from being prosperous. It is also possible for covetousness to develop once we enjoy prosperity.

Jesus told a parable that illustrated this:

> Then one from the crowd said to Him, "Teacher, tell my brother to divide the inheritance with me." But He said to him, "Man, who made Me a judge or an arbitrator over you?" And He said to them, "Take heed and beware of covetousness, for one's life does not consist in the abundance of the things he possesses." Then He spoke a parable to them, saying: "The ground of a certain rich man yielded plentifully. And he thought within himself, saying, 'What shall I do, since I have no room to store my crops?' So he said, 'I will do this: I will pull down my barns and build greater, and there I will store all my crops and my goods. And I will say to my soul, "Soul, you have many goods laid up for many years; take your ease; eat, drink, and be merry."' But God said to him, 'Fool! This night your soul will be required of you; then whose will those things be which you have provided?' So is he who lays up treasure for himself, and is not rich toward God" (Luke 12:13–21).

Note the context for this parable. A man came to Jesus asking Jesus to tell his brother to divide an inheritance with him. The man who came to Jesus was very likely a younger brother, and the inheritance was likely the inheritance that went to the eldest brother—which was double the inheritance received by the other brothers. The younger brother no doubt wanted more than he was owed under the law of Moses; in other words, he was asking for something that was not rightfully his. He wanted the reward of more inheritance without the responsibility that went with it.

(The double inheritance to a firstborn son also carried with it many family responsibilities.)

Jesus could tell that the man's request—wanting something for nothing—was rooted in covetousness. The same is true for any person who wants something for nothing. She is greedy. She covets what is not rightfully hers—what she has not earned, what she does not deserve, what she has not been given.

The greedy, covetous person begins to think that his possessions are not only his security but also his very identity. His portfolio—his wealth, his bank statements, his possessions—say to the world and to himself, "Look who I am."

Your identity is always to be in Christ Jesus, not in things, status, or other relationships. A covetous spirit moves you away from intimacy with God and into a state of pride, which is the second attitude you must avoid.

- *In your experience, have you ever known a person whose greed, or covetous spirit, led to a loss of prosperity?*

_____

_____

2. Pride

The parable that Jesus taught in response to the encounter with the covetous brother speaks directly to the dangers of pride. Reread the passage from Luke. Circle the words *I* and *my* as you read the verses.

The proud person believes that he has earned all that he has; therefore, he has sole right to what he has. Jesus taught first that the rich man in this parable had great wealth because his land "yielded plentifully." It was a good year for farming; however, he saw the crops as *his* crops, the barns as *his* barns, all of the income as *his* income. There was no mention of giving God the firstfruits of the harvest, or any portion of it. He was totally self-contained and self-absorbed. He spoke totally to himself, about himself.

When you begin to take pride in your prosperity, you discount or eliminate the recognition and praise belonging to God. You take credit for an achievement that is not totally your own. You rob God of the tithe and offerings owed to God, and you presume to rob God of the glory owed His name.

God will not prosper anyone who presumes to take for herself the praise that is rightfully God's alone.

3. Selfishness

The rich man in the parable became selfish. He hoarded what he had. His possessions began to possess him.

Selfish people rarely are generous toward God. I have met very few selfish people who tithe regularly; if they tithe, they do so grudgingly and without joy, and they reap virtually no emotional or spiritual blessing from their giving.

We all know what happens to a lake that has no outlet. It becomes slimy, and eventually, all life within it is killed. The selfish person gradually dies on the inside, and his prosperity grows stale and withers away.

4. Presumption

Prosperous people must also guard against becoming presumptuous, which is an attitude that says, "I am owed this prosperity." They think that they have earned prosperity or that they are deserving of prosperity because of something they have done or are.

God delights in giving to you, but at no time is He indebted to you. You must remain humble at all times, recognizing that all your life, including every breath you take, every beat of your heart, and every moment you live, is according to God's grace and will. God is never required to serve you; at all times you are His servant.

Presumption is a close cousin to pride.

5. Pleasure

The rich man in Jesus' parable said, "Soul, you have many goods laid up for many years; take your ease; eat, drink, and be merry."

The man decided to take his prosperity and live off it for the rest of his life. He had no desire to put forth any more effort. There is no mention of any desire to work for God. He wanted an easy life. He erroneously presumed that he had many years to live out the life of leisure that he envisioned for himself.

God responded, "Fool! This night your soul will be required of you; then whose will those things be which you have provided?"

No one can count on tomorrow. Our time on this earth is in God's hands. We are to work with all of our energy and ability every day of our lives—regardless of the amount of energy and ability we may have at any given point. If we are not working in a career that produces income for ourselves, we certainly should be active in a volunteer job or ministry that benefits others. There is no retirement from being a productive member of the kingdom of God or from being an active witness to God's love.

- *Have you ever known anyone who lost prosperity as the result of pride, selfishness, presumption, or a desire to live only for personal pleasure?*

_____

_____

The rich man in Jesus' parable lost out materially and spiritually. God called him a fool.

Ask the Lord to help you stay free of the following:

- A covetous spirit
- Pride
- Selfishness or self-centeredness
- Presumption that God owes you prosperity
- A desire to live only for your ease, comfort, or pleasure

People who begin to have these attitudes are in danger of having their possessions possess them, their goals become their gods, and their desires destroy them.

What the Word Says	What the Word Says to Me
A faithful man will abound with blessings, But he who hastens to be rich will not go unpunished (Prov. 28:20).	_____ _____ _____ _____ _____

Better is the poor who walks in
his integrity
Than one perverse in his ways,
though he be rich (Prov. 28:6).

_____
_____
_____
_____

He who covers his sins will not
prosper,
But whoever confesses and for-
sakes them will have mercy
(Prov. 28:13).

_____
_____
_____
_____
_____

You ask and do not receive, because you ask amiss, that you
may spend it on your pleasures
(James 4:3).

_____
_____
_____
_____

Five Warning Signs You Must Heed

You are in danger of losing your prosperity if any one of these
five conditions begins to characterize your life:

*1. You no longer consider money to be for the sustenance of life; rather,
money becomes the consistency of your life.* You do not use money
merely to sustain your life; your life begins to consist of abundance
of possessions that you constantly think about acquiring or main-
taining.

I once heard about a man who concluded that he truly no longer
had room enough to contain all of God's blessings. He found that
he was occupied virtually all the time with concerns about the
maintenance of his three homes and five automobiles, not to
mention his fishing and ski boats, his two snowmobiles, and his
co-ownership of a small airplane. Something always seemed to
need repair, preventive maintenance, a tune-up, or a remodeling
job. He said, "There wasn't much time left for anything else except
to be concerned about taxes and which expenses could be de-
ducted. I decided to eliminate at least half of what I had owned in
order to have time to enjoy the other half!" The consistency of the

man's life had become wrapped up in things. He was wise to get rid of what he did.

You must never allow your possessions to grow beyond the sustenance level. When all of your plans and ambitions are related to material goods, you are in danger.

2. *You begin to fall in love with money.* Nobody sets out to love money. People usually drift into that position slowly and imperceptibly. Be aware of your growing desires for certain objects or a growing obsession to meet certain financial goals, including sales quotas and profit margins.

Falling in love with money includes falling in love with the idea of making money and with the things money can buy. You daydream constantly about the things you would like to own, and your mind is preoccupied with get-rich schemes and your plans to increase your income.

The love of money leads to compromise of values. It leads to cutting corners in other important areas of your life so you can devote more time and energy to your job or to consumerism.

When you begin to love money, you are in danger. The Bible teaches, "The love of money is a root of all kinds of evil, for which some have strayed from the faith in their greediness, and pierced themselves through with many sorrows" (1 Tim. 6:10).

We know that a love of money can result in the evil of crime. However, many evils that come from a love of money are much more subtle than that. Some of the sorrows may be feelings of

- inner emptiness.
- disillusionment.
- disappointment.
- deep inner dissatisfaction.
- nagging frustrations and worries.

The sorrows may include destroyed relationships with business colleagues and associates as well as family members. The sorrows may include a loss of intimacy with God.

- *Based on your experience, what other sorrows may occur for people who begin to love money?*

_____

_____

3. You set out to be rich. Gaining wealth becomes your number one goal. When the acquisition of money and material goods becomes the foremost ambition of your life, you are in danger. First Timothy 6:9 warns, "Those who desire to be rich fall into temptation and a snare, and into many foolish and harmful lusts which drown men in destruction and perdition."

If you want more than anything else to be wealthy, you become a prime target for every illegal or immoral money-making scheme that comes along. Your judgment will be clouded regarding business associates. Your common sense will evaporate. You will be prone to temptation.

4. You become reckless in the handling of a blessing of money that may come your way. When an unexpected financial blessing occurs, or when financial blessings begin to accumulate beyond a sustenance level, the tendency of some people is to hoard that money, while the tendency of others is to spend that money with freewheeling abandon. Both positions are dangerous.

The Lord desires for you to be generous. He also desires for you to be prudent. Give tithes and offerings to God's storehouse. Set aside a reasonable amount in savings. Invest wisely. Spend wisely.

5. You look to your financial concerns more than to God's Word in making key decisions in your life. Let me share some very practical specific ways in which this may manifest itself:

- You visualize what money can do for you more than what God can do for you.
- You plan your life around your income instead of what God calls you to do.
- You start to feel that you have no time to hear God's Word or to participate in church or ministry activities.

- You look for get-rich schemes and rationalize why they might be good for you.
- You work for retirement ease rather than retirement service.
- You begin to designate certain possessions as solely for your personal use.
- You have a growing discontent with the possessions you have, and a growing desire for things you don't own.
- You spend more of your off-work time with people who are involved in your business or money-making endeavors than with your family and church friends.
- Your desire moves away from spending time with God to spending time dealing with money, investments, or new business ventures.

Pay attention to these warning signs. Refuse to yield to them.

If you find that you are starting to develop these patterns in your life, ask God to forgive you and to help you return to the principles and habits that brought you to a prosperous position in life in the first place. Trust Him anew with your whole life, and ask Him to restore to you a balance of wholeness and prosperity that is first and foremost spiritual prosperity.

- *What new insights do you have into God's plan for keeping the prosperity He gives you?*

_____

_____

- *In what ways is God challenging you today?*

_____

_____

LESSON 10

THE WHEEL OF PROSPERITY

God intends for you to live a positive life in a negative world. He wants you to prosper.

Why aren't more people prosperous in the totality of their lives?

Part of the reason is tradition. People tend to be creatures of habits, some of which are long-standing. Tradition can be either a trap or a blessing. Jesus wasn't accepted as Messiah because the religious leaders of His day were locked into traditional beliefs that did not allow for a suffering, self-sacrificing, spiritual Messiah. They were seeking a triumphant political leader, and their beliefs blinded them to the truth of Jesus as their Redeemer.

Part of the reason more people don't experience prosperity is that people tend to gravitate toward what is safe, not necessarily what is good. Those who experience good often settle for good rather than pursuing what is better or best.

To be prosperous—to receive and enjoy ongoing blessings in every area of your life—you have to *want* to be prosperous. You have to want to live your life in obedience to God's plan and principles, and you have to want more for every area of your life, especially more for your spiritual life and your witness for Christ. When you truly desire to be prosperous and you turn to God and ask Him to lead you into the way of total prosperity that He has designed for you, I believe you have taken a major step toward prosperity. God answers and more than satisfies the heart that is hungry for Him and a life lived according to His will.

God's desire for you to prosper has been a recurring message throughout these lessons. If you have any remaining doubt that God wants to bless you, or that He will bless you if you live your life in line with His plan and principles for prosperity, I encourage you to reread the verses in this study guide and also read the verses below.

What the Word Says	What the Word Says to Me
This Book of the Law shall not depart from your mouth, but you shall meditate in it day and night, that you may observe to do according to all that is written in it. For then you will make your way prosperous, and then you will have good success. Have I not commanded you? Be strong and of good courage; do not be afraid, nor be dismayed, for the LORD your God is with you wherever you go (Josh. 1:8–9).	_____
Blessed is the man Who walks not in the counsel of the ungodly, Nor stands in the path of sinners, Nor sits in the seat of the scornful; But his delight is in the law of the LORD, And in His law he meditates day and night.	_____

He shall be like a tree   _____
Planted by the rivers of water,   _____
That brings forth its fruit in its   _____
season,
Whose leaf also shall not wither;   _____
And whatever he does shall pros-   _____
per.   _____
The ungodly are not so,   _____
But are like the chaff which the   _____
wind drives away.   _____
Therefore the ungodly shall not   _____
stand in the judgment,   _____
Nor sinners in the congregation   _____
of the righteous.   _____
For the LORD knows the way of   _____
the righteous,   _____
But the way of the ungodly shall   _____
perish (Ps. 1).   _____

As you open up yourself to God's plan for prosperity, I encourage you to do something that is very practical and visual: make a wheel of prosperity.

Making a Prosperity Wheel

Get a large piece of paper, and draw as large a circle as you can on it. Inside the circle, at its center, draw a smaller circle. Label the smaller circle "God." Then draw crosshairs over the large circle so that you have divided the large circle (and the smaller one embedded in it) into four even quadrants. Label these four sections: "Family Life," "Social/Recreational Life," "Business Life," and "Spiritual Life."

Next I encourage you to identify goals for each area of your life. If you don't set your goals, someone else will set them for you.

Don't write down your goals using words. Instead, use pictures. Find pictures in magazines and so forth that illustrate what you want. For example, if you want to study the Bible more, find a picture of a Bible or a picture of someone reading the Bible. If you want to spend more time with your family, find a picture of family members doing something together. If you can't find a picture that fits your goal, draw a picture the best you can.

After you have completed your wheel, put it in a place where you can refer to it often, such as the inside of a closet door. If you desire for your wheel to remain private and personal, put it in a place "for your eyes only," perhaps a locked desk drawer.

Encourage other members of your family to make wheels of prosperity for their individual lives. (Your children might label the "Business Life" quadrant as "School Life.") And then come together as a family to make a wheel of prosperity that pertains to your family life as a whole. You may find that many of your goals in each quadrant of your life are shared by other family members. Pray together as a family about which goals are most important to you.

Benefits from the Wheel

What does a wheel like this do for you?

First, a wheel of prosperity will remind you continually to keep God at the center of your desires. The wheel will remind you always that God is the Source of your whole-life prosperity. Seeing the word *God* in the midst of your goals will remind you that all of your ability, resources, talent, and time comes from God. It will also remind you to ask God often to direct your goal setting, and to help you achieve the goals that you truly conclude are God-ordained, God-authorized, or God-approved.

Second, a wheel of prosperity is likely to compel you to adjust priorities in your life. If you see that you have many goals in one area of your life, but very few in another, you must face the fact that your life is lopsided. A wheel that is out of balance results in a bumpy ride! Furthermore, a wheel that is out of balance creates a wobble that will eventually cause the wheel to break apart. Take a good look at what you desire. Make all of these goals a matter of prayer priority. As the Lord leads you and directs you, change your priorities and readjust your goals, perhaps coming up with new or replacement goals, until you feel your wheel is balanced and approved by God.

As you look at your wheel of prosperity, begin by looking at the word *God* and spend a few moments dwelling on the goodness of God and His many benefits to you. Give Him thanks and praise. Ask Him to direct your attention to areas of your life that need adjustment. As your eyes scan your wheel, you are likely to feel drawn to a particular goal or activity. Ask the Lord to give you His wisdom about this area of your life.

Third, a wheel of prosperity allows you to take a look at your total life at a glance. When I made my first wheel of prosperity I realized as never before that I had very few social and recreational activities or goals. That realization helped me face the fact that I was headed for stress overload or burnout. If someone had asked me, "Do you lead a balanced life?" I would have answered, "Sure I do." But seeing my wheel of prosperity out of balance made me reevaluate my use of time and resources, as well as my hopes, desires, and goals.

After you have made your wheel of prosperity, answer these questions:

- *How do I feel about the balance of my wheel?*

  _____

  _____

- *In my past experience, which area of my life have I tended to emphasize? Neglect? With what results?*

  _____

  _____

- *What new insights do I have into God's desire for me to be a whole person and to prosper in the totality of my life?*

  _____

  _____

• *In what ways am I being challenged by God today?*

_____

_____

Managing the Wheel

A wheel of prosperity helps in five ways:

1. Visualization. The wheel is based on the goodness of God and the goodness of His blessings to His people. Remind yourself always as you look at your wheel of prosperity that "the earth is full of the goodness of the LORD" (Ps. 33:5). Ask the Lord to rule your imagination and to provide a glimpse of His plan for you and the blessings He desires to give to you.

2. Expectation. The wheel is based on the promises of God. The Bible declares that "you do not have because you do not ask" (James 4:2). As you visualize and identify your goals, you are in a better position to ask God specifically for what you truly desire and then to look for His answer or provision.

3. Motivation. The wheel is based on the plan of God. Psalm 32:8 states,

> *I will instruct you and teach you in the way you should go;*
> *I will guide you with My eye.*

Make it your motivation to see your life as God sees it, and then to do what God instructs and guides you to do. Make Psalm 25:4–5 your prayer:

> *Show me Your ways, O LORD;*
> *Teach me Your paths.*
> *Lead me in Your truth and teach me,*
> *For You are the God of my salvation;*
> *On You I wait all the day.*

4. Meditation. The wheel is based on submission to God. As you meditate on God's Word, you learn more about the goodness of

God and the goodness of His plan for your life. You must line up your personal plans and desires against the absolutes of God's Word. As 1 Thessalonians 5:21–22 admonishes, you must "test all things; hold fast what is good. Abstain from every form of evil." If at any time you find a Scripture that identifies one of your goals as being wrong before the Lord, you must remove it from your wheel.

5. *Realization.* The wheel is based on the faithfulness of God to be true to His Word that He will guide you into all truth, He will impart to you His wisdom, and He will act for your eternal good. Remind yourself of God's promise: "All things work together for good to those who love God, to those who are the called according to His purpose" (Rom. 8:28).

A wheel of prosperity can help you open yourself to God and develop a greater dependency on Him. That's one of the reasons I encourage you to construct it as a circle. Let it remind you always of God's desire that you be whole. Prosperity is rooted always in wholeness, growth, and fruitfulness.

It is not enough to believe in prosperity, believe for prosperity, or visualize prosperity. Eventually, you must do the things the Lord calls you to do. You must actually live out His plan. I encourage you to take that step today!

- *In what ways are you being challenged to act on God's plan for prosperity for your life?*

_____

_____

EPILOGUE

MY FINAL WORD TO YOU

I f I could leave you with only three main concepts about financial stewardship, they would be these:

1. God desires to prosper you. He is a God of infinite goodness who desires only your best. God's foremost desire is that you believe in His Son, Jesus Christ, and receive God's forgiveness for your sins. All other aspects of prosperity flow from that decision in your life.

2. Prosperity is not limited to your finances, although it includes your finances. Prosperity involves your entire life; it is a life of wholeness, growth, and blessing for your spirit, mind, emotions, relationships, and material existence.

3. For you to experience prosperity, you must obey God's plan and principles as set forth in His Word. In the area of financial stewardship, obedience includes a desire and willingness to work, a desire and plan of action for getting out of debt, and your tithes and offerings delivered into God's storehouse on a consistent basis. Acting on your faith is a form of obedience. You must believe that God is and always will be true to His Word and that He is utterly faithful and trustworthy.

No one can do your believing for you. Nobody can do your obeying for you. Nobody else can give what you uniquely have to give. The prosperity God has for you is 100 percent tailor-made for you. It is a unique prosperity suited for God's unique purpose for your life.

Finally, God requires your participation in order for you to receive the prosperity He has for you. God extends an offer of prosperity. It is up to you to act on that offer and actively receive all that God desires to give. In return, He stands eager to receive all of you to Himself.

Prosperity is rooted and established in your having a relationship with God. The deeper and more intimate your relationship with Him, the greater your capacity to receive and experience prosperity. The more you love God and receive His love, the greater the wholeness, the greater the joy.

God longs for you to understand and engage in sound financial stewardship. Even more so, He longs for you to experience wholeness. And even more so, He longs for you to know Him.